STEPPARENTING

THE REAL PROBLEMS • THE REAL SOLUTIONS

REVISED AND UPDATED

JEANNETTE LOFAS, CSW, WITH DAWN B. SOVA

MJF Books
New York

Published by MJF Books
Fine Communications
Two Lincoln Square
60 West 66th Street
New York, NY 10023

Stepparenting
Library of Congress Catalog Card Number #97-72762
ISBN 1-56731-179-2

Manufactured in the United States of America on acid-free paper

MJF Books and the MJF colophon are trademarks of Fine Creative Media, Inc.

10 9 8 7 6 5 4 3 2 1

To my family, friends, and staff, who lovingly nurtured me through the writing of this book and the battles we have fought to bring step relationships to the public consciousness. With special thanks to Ian McDonald, our operations manager at the Stepfamily Foundation, for his intelligent and vital assistance.

To all those who live in stepfamilies, whether married or living together. I hope we have helped to make their lives and their children's lives just a bit easier.

CONTENTS

INTRODUCTION

I write this book as one who has lived in stepfamily relationships most of my life. However, until I married a man with four daughters—I was divorced with a son of my own—I, like most people, lived in complete denial about "step." Despite the fact that my mother and father had divorced, both had remarried, and I had one brother, two half-brothers, and three stepsisters, at no time had I even thought of the word "step," or seen myself as a stepchild!

Stepfamilies are now the norm. The typical fifties family of biological father, homemaking mother, and two children is virtually nonexistent. We are a nation of divorced individuals. Today's typical family is *not* the first family, the biologically connected nuclear family or intact family, as it is variously labeled. The majority of today's families include a step relationship in one form or another. It may be a remarried family or a living-together family system with biological parent, partner, and child.

"Step" is generally handled by denial. And so are its problems. The result is that two out of three step relationships with children break up. The children of divorce, remarriage, and redivorce undergo the most self-esteem battering and loss of self-worth that they will experience in a lifetime.

It doesn't have to be this way.

Mythology Is Everywhere

A divorced mom or dad may say, "I'm not in a stepfamily! Oh, sure, I date and my ex is remarried, but it's not a stepfamily!" That's the first big myth. The fact is, all of you are now part of an extended stepfamily: custodial parent, visiting parent, and all new significant others.

I remarried with the second classic myth: Love me, love my child. Love him, love his children. Was I off-base on that one!

I had come out of nineteen years of TV news. Plane crashes, assassinations—nothing, *nothing* was harder than when my husband's kids would come to visit. He would turn into an overindulgent wimp doing everything for his girls, and I would turn into a snarling tiger mother defending my small son from my husband's putdowns. Something was tremendously wrong. What happened to our love?

So what does a reporter do with a problem? She seeks experts. I went to the library, only to discover literally a single book on this subject, written by a stepmother complaining how awful it was. There was a gaping hole that had to be filled. With Ruth Roosevelt, I wrote the first book about step relationships, *Living In Step, a Remarriage Manual,* in 1976 (McGraw Hill, New York).

During the course of our research we interviewed every top therapist in the country. In reality, we didn't learn much from these nationwide "experts." Then, and sadly, still today, most psychiatrists, psychologists, and social workers were trained in the model of the intact or biologically connected family. We listened to their well-intentioned advice and knew it had little application for the stepfamily. It was simply not relevant. Not surprisingly, we learned much more from the hundreds of stepfamilies we interviewed.

In 1975 I incorporated the Stepfamily Foundation, Inc. Since that time I have counseled thousands of families and trained over three thousand therapists and clergy.

We offer a methodology that works.

Chapter 1

WHAT IS STEP?

I choose to use the word "step," rather than such terms as "blended" or "reconstituted" families which are more frequently used. Many people refuse to use the word "step" because it calls to mind a host of ugly myths—the wicked stepchildren, the cruel stepmothers, the evil stepfathers of fairy tales. It seems easier to use a more pleasant-sounding term and leave it at that. However, a step situation isn't blended or reconstituted. The two families, parents and children in whatever combination, do not mix and merge and become indistinguishable from each other. Even to suggest that they should is an insult to the individuals that make up those families. Instead they combine—often with great difficulty—bringing with them their past and complicated dynamics that must be integrated, and honored, to create a new family paradigm . . . the *step*family.

What Makes a Step Relationship?

"Step" relationships occur after the divorce of a couple or the death of a spouse and when there are children from the prior relationship. Heterosexual couple or homosexual couple, married or living together, when children from a prior relationship are involved you've got a step relationship on your hands. And that means you have to work harder to make your relationship with your new partner a success.

Today 70 million Americans live in some form of step relationship. They may live with someone else's children. They may live with their own children with a new partner. They may be dating someone with children. They may be the noncustodial parent whose prior spouse has remarried. And, of course, they may be the children themselves. These children have suffered the breakup of their family, and often are not easy children.

Whatever their role, these people often feel that they can nonchalantly enter a step relationship and leave it to develop on its own. Those who deny, their heads firmly entrenched in the sand, may well fail. The success stories involve those families who acknowledge the difficulties of step relationships and decide to confront and to solve the challenges of step.

There is far too much denial among the step population. Surveys and direct observations show that step relationships may well be one of the most endangered species among relationships. Statistically, the divorce rate among step marriages is higher than the overall remarriage divorce rate. As to other step relationships, no firm figures are possible. Living-together step relationships and dating step relationships die silent deaths, leaving no divorce statistics.

Because one or both of the new partners involved in step have an all too recent history of either death or divorce, step relationships often begin with heightened sensitivity and shaky resolve. This is aggravated when the family tries desperately to view itself in the same light as the traditional intact family—a very common mistake among individuals in step. That's the bad news.

The good news is that if you confront the reality of the situation and identify your problems, there's no reason why your step relationship can't be a success. That is the major goal of the Stepfamily Foundation. It is also the goal of this book. In the chapters that follow, you will learn to deal with the problems that are unique to step. You will learn techniques for dating, for debugging the relationship, for organizing the household, for dealing with the rituals and the etiquette and the daily practical needs of step relationships.

Most important, you will begin to uncover the hidden strengths of your particular stepfamily. Your new skills will help you to see each new difficulty for what it is—a situation, often classic to step, to be handled with knowledge and love, and with the welfare of your stepfamily always prominent in your mind.

Does that mean that you will never have another problem in the step relationship once you have taken care of those that you have now? Not at all. There is no such thing as life without conflict. What it does mean is that you will have the tools at hand to solve your problems and keep your step relationship healthy.

The Statistics Are Staggering

The numbers tell the story: *The American family as we knew it is no longer.*

The current American family has become a high-risk stepfamily system; 1300 new stepfamilies are forming every day.

Step systems are created after the death of the intact family and begin as soon as the single parent is dating, living with a partner, or is remarried. These relationships fail at the rate of two out of three, dramatically affecting all involved . . . especially the children, the most precious resources of this society. The emotional viability of these children is endangered.

The average marriage in America lasts only seven years. Statistically, one out of two marriages ends in divorce. By the year 2000 there will be more stepfamilies than original families; 59 percent of children will live in a stepfamily before reaching age 18; 50 percent of children will live significant periods of their formative years without a father (ten-year projections say 60 percent).

A study found that in the year following divorce women with children averaged a 73 percent drop in their standard of living, while their husbands averaged a 42 percent rise; 52 percent of divorced fathers with a legal agreement pay the full child support amount, 23 percent pay partial support, and 21 percent pay nothing at all. The average amount paid to a divorced women and the children is $2,710 a year.

Think about it! Only 5.7 percent of the 83,500,000 households in the U.S. consist of the "nuclear" family, a working father, homemaking mother, and two or more children.

What does all this mean? It means that most children today live in step relationships, of which two out of three are predicted to fail. This family failure causes the child to lack the crucial support that enables him to thrive or even survive society's cultural, educational, and work systems.

In her famous book *Second Chances,* Judith Wallerstein, Ph.D., details the effects on children of divorce, in a ten-to-fifteen-year study of *middle- and upper-*class children of divorce. The working-class and lower-class children have not been studied. We can only imagine the effects on them.

Wallerstein reports that only 45 percent of children "do well after divorce. . . . 41% are doing poorly, worried, underachieving, deprecating, and often angry." Fifty percent of the women and 30 percent of the men were still intensely angry at their former spouses. "Most felt the lack of a template, a working model, for a loving relationship between a man and a woman."

Studies show that divorced parents provide less time, less discipline, and are less sensitive to the children as they are caught up in their own divorce and its aftermath. Many parents are unable to separate their needs from the children's needs and often share too much of their personal life with their children, placing the children in a precarious emotional state, vulnerable to grandiosity or to depression within what is left of their families. The majority of parents of divorce are chronically disorganized and unable to parent effectively. As diminished parenting continues, it permanently disrupts the child's once normal emotional growth and functioning.

The good news, according to the study: "The children of divorce tended to do well if mothers and father, regardless of remarriage, resumed parenting roles, putting differences aside, and allowing the children continuing relationships with both parents. Only a few children had these advantages."

Huge Increase in Living-Together Stepfamilies

In his 1994 study, "The Changing Character of Stepfamilies," Professor of Sociology Larry L. Bumpass of the University of Wisconsin challenges the common perception that the stepfamily is defined by marriage. His research states that about half of the 60 million children under the age of thirteen in this country are currently *living with* one biological parent and that parent's current partner. He declares that nearly half of all women, not just mothers, are likely to live in a stepfamily relationship, when we include living-together families in our definition of the stepfamily.

Bumpass further found that most parents of preschoolers who live in stepfamilies are living with a partner to whom they are not married. At least a quarter of stepfamilies involve couples who live together and at least half of currently married stepfamilies began with a living-together situation before they married.

What do these numbers mean? They mean that we must rethink our perceptions of the American family. We must acknowledge that when a biological parent lives with his/her child and partner, they are living in a stepfamily regardless of marriage or any other civil registration. In other words, documents do not make families.

Millions of these families exist, and they have a higher chance of failure than any other type of family. We must view Professor Bumpass's work as a call to arms. If we continue to ignore these families and their solvable problems, we will continue to undermine the integrity of the American family and, perhaps worst of all, ignore the needs of over 25 million children.

Chapter 2

THE MAN AND WOMAN IN STEP

Today we are witnessing one of the most powerful movements in the history of mankind. It certainly is no less significant than the Industrial Revolution or World War II.

Men and women in step must take into consideration the momentous shifts that have taken place in society in relation to women's roles, men's roles, and the position of children in the family. It is the result of the women's movement and the divorce epidemic. It is the new American family: the stepfamily.

Today we see both male and female competing for control. To build the couple strength, it is often important to put aside our egos. Parental discord in front of the children has always been ill-advised. In step it happens more often and is even more destructive, shaking the already precarious step structure. Disputes in front of the children allow space for the children to wedge in between the couple.

Such discord can be avoided. This is not to say partnership is built on the male and the female repressing whatever their viewpoints might be. But it is to say that we might need to reevaluate our current notions. There are alternatives to flight, fight, and fuming.

It takes a commitment to each other and a commitment to learning "how to partner" as a man and a woman. If there is any one lesson we try to teach our clients, it is this. We must be steadfast in holding the vision of the kind of relationship we want. We must not be deterred by the barriers others may put between us and this vision. Either the barriers run our relationship or we hold our vision and move toward it. We have a choice—to focus our lives on the barriers or on the vision. So many people spend their lives responding to negativity rather than assuming the responsibility of creating what they want.

An ancient philosopher said: "So a man thinketh, so he is."

However, most couples in step, when they first come to the Stepfamily Foundation, have a similar and predictable litany of complaints. These complaints are not without foundation. They are classic to step. We need to know what they are before we can do something about them.

The Fathers of Divorce and Step: Classic Complaints

- She knew I had children when she married me, so why does she act this way *now?*
- In so much of what she says to the children there is an edge of nastiness in her voice.
- She acts more like a child than they do.
- She wants a baby and she can't even handle my children.
- She's obsessed by everything my former wife does.
- Will she ever understand how hard it is on a man to lose his children?
- Will she ever know how haunted I am by the guilt of not being there?

• Can't she just respect that the notion of "quality time" is just not enough?

• How can she expect me to discipline them when I see them so little?

• I'm afraid they will go and never come back if I start punishing them.

• She see things they do that I never see.

• Sometimes I think she is looking to find the worse in them.

• Sure my ex-wife has control over me: She controls my children.

• My ex makes me out to be the monster, when she wanted the divorce.

• My money can never go far enough. Nor is it ever in the right place.

• Sometimes I get so hurt by her leaving all day Saturday and expecting me to take the children out to dinner alone. But if I say anything she'll probably be there even less.

Some Data

One out of two fathers will divorce, and only 1 percent will receive custody of their children, unless later widowed. One of four men stop seeing their children. The ex may bad-mouth him, the kids lose interest, and, finally, after numerous attempts and even court battles, the father gives up. Approximately half of divorced fathers do not pay child support, or pay only part of it. However, many single and remarried men are visiting and fathering their children.

As a group, divorced men with children are dreadfully misunderstood by society. They are often branded as deserters, irresponsible males who have walked away from their children. More often than not these fathers have not left their children; many spend hours on the road to visit them and go out of their way to maintain a relationship.

Many have to be satisfied with hit-or-miss relationships. They see their kids, if at all, as the mother and child choose. Often Dad feels that no matter what he gives the child, the relationship is empty.

The good news: We are now seeing increasing numbers of these men in our Stepfamily Foundation counseling rooms. The reason? They want to be the best fathers they can, and realize they need to know more and do more to maintain their family role.

The Male Way of Being

Fathers have a special responsibility to their sons. After puberty women cannot teach young males the rules of a man's universe: team sports, taking orders from the boss, following the task through, and not quitting. In our society it is sometimes okay for young girls to quit the game. For boys, quitting, not completing the task, or accepting their rank in the pecking order with older males, will diminish their chances in the male-dominated hierarchy they'll face as men.

Girls must also learn some of these rules from Dad. They, too, will have to compete in the masculine workplace. A girl's healthy relationship with Dad also leads to better relationships with men later on.

Howie, the Mega-wimp Father

Howard is a strikingly good-looking and successful forty-four-year-old investment banker. Daily, he wheels and deals with powerful moneyed clients. Indeed, at work he is the cock of the walk.

But at home Howard—whom his kids call Howie—is a mega-wimp.

Howard is a divorced man, the father of Judy, a twelve-year old, and Jason, who just turned eight. Both youngsters live with Howard's ex-wife, a woman he views as a bad-mouthing shrew unfit to be a mother. If he's lucky, he may see his children two weekends a month.

Angry, worried, and guilt-ridden, Howard is determined to be their best pal and make every visit a thrill a minute, shuttling them from theme park to mall to movie. Instead of giving them tasks, teaching them discipline and values, he showers the kids with gifts. At home he becomes their butler, maid, and cook, all wrapped into one. Throughout most of these visits, Judy and Jason alternatively run amuck, outshouting each other or sitting passively on the couch, staring at cartoons with vacant expressions.

Like many of today's divorced men with children, Howard is part of a phenomenon known as Disneyland Daddies—a new brand of fathers who feel powerless to perform and thus overlook many of their fathering responsibilities. The result is essentially the "unfathered child."

A divorced man who just provides dinner, some small talk, or a sporting event for his children is not a father. He is Daddy-as-entertainment-center. He is a do-me-buy-me-drive-me Daddy. The bottom line: He is not providing a home for his children or building an intimate connection. This connection with the father helps kids to grow up whole, with self-esteem and knowledge of how the man's world works.

Mr. Mom and the Stepmother

When you are the visiting biological father of the children, you have to assume a new role. No longer is being "dad" enough; the day-to-day functions of mothering have entered into the picture. The father with visitation must learn to tie shoelaces, keep track of mittens, teach manners, build self-esteem, set boundaries, and make dinner—sometimes all at the same time. This can be difficult, as most men are programmed to do one thing at a time, complete it, and go on to the next.

So many stepmothers complain that the father doesn't even seem to notice that the kids are loud and unruly, that their hands are dirty and they are eating junk food. And it's true; he often doesn't notice. That was never in his job description. This was not his role. He was solely the hunter/warrior. The mother taught and cared for the kids. However, in this new age of divorce, it *is* his job. Simply because the stepmother sees what is going on, she must not be the one to initiate and manage discipline.

If you are a divorced father and find that your new wife is constantly complaining about the behavior of your children, ask her to point out specific things and discuss them with her—but not in front of the children. Remember, the couple must resolve these issues. Kids can feel and see dissension between the couple. Stepkids will contribute to it—indeed, cultivate it, working to drive a wedge between the couple. A lack of couple strength can impair the child's sense of his world as a stable place and, more important, his sense of self.

I Am the King

Sam was just below the level of tycoon in the publishing business. He was forty-two, good-looking, successful, and divorced with two children. The children came every other weekend. There was young Sammy, fifteen, and Mary Ellen, eleven. Sam was seriously dating Linda, a thirty-six-year-old, never-married book editor. Although they still had separate homes, they spent a lot of time together. Sam loved Linda, but he didn't know if he could endure her endless complaints about his children: how he spoiled them and didn't teach them anything.

When Sam came in to see us he was just looking for some advice to ascertain whether he was handling his divorce and the kids all right. He didn't invite Linda to come to the first session.

Sam told us how his wife had wanted the divorce and that she had a drinking problem. He wanted to see the children as much as possible and felt that they weren't getting the kind of quality parenting from their mother that he could give them. I asked him about his routine with his children. He said that on Friday nights they usually went out to dinner. Linda seldom came because the kids didn't like her and were often very rude to her. On Saturdays he made them breakfast, lunch, and dinner and took them to various activities and events that he had planned with them. Saturday-night dinners, both he and Linda cooked . . . most of the time. They would spend the late-afternoon shopping, and even if Linda wasn't there, Sam would cook, serve, and clean up. Sometimes the kids insisted upon watching television at dinner, but not always.

He felt that since he had the kids for only four days a month the last thing he wanted to do was make their lives more difficult or unhappy. He was afraid that would only succeed in making them not want to see him at all. As a result, Sam didn't ask them to help in any way. In fact, the children often told *him* what they needed from the kitchen—they expected him to get it instead of getting it themselves. So here was tycoon Sam being the do-good Daddy, the servant on weekends. His actions are classic for all too many divorced Dads.

Sam also related that his son Sammy called Linda a "bimbo," usually not to her face but under his breath. Sam said he didn't want to squelch the child's freedom of expression. "After all, children have a right to their opinions, don't they?"

Toward the end of the first session I asked Sam what he was teaching his children.

"That they are loved," answered Sam. "That this is a good place for them to be." I then asked him if he would hire Sammy to work in his office. Sam looked startled. "Well . . . er . . . um . . . he can behave himself when he wants to . . . but he doesn't around me."

I told Sam that fathering is about teaching children, especially boy children, the ways of men in the world . . . and the ways of hierarchy and order in general and in the business world in particular.

"We have a young man here who knows how to express himself but has no idea how to relate in the real world," I pointed out to him. "He sits and watches television while you work all day and then serve him on the weekends. Is it the maid and butler's role that you want to teach him? You have become the maid and butler to this child, and you do him a great disservice in not teaching him the hierarchy of male rankings and acceptable relationships between senior and junior males. He is not receiving the tools that he needs to go out and make it in a competitive male world."

Sam looked quite pale and said, "What do I do?"

"Do you really want to know?" I asked. "Do you really want to teach this boy?"

"Yes, yes, I do," said Sam. "Yes, yes, I need to."

"You know," I said, "you won't lose him if you teach him. You may lose him more if you don't teach him. So here's what you do:

"You need quiet time to talk with him without distractions, perhaps after a meal together. Linda shouldn't be present. You say, 'You are the prince. You are my immortality. You are my firstborn son. I will do everything I can to make life good for you. But I am the king. The king runs the kingdom and the king teaches the prince discipline and honor and being gentlemanly even when we don't like someone. The king is the top of the hierarchy and the prince is below. And so, young man, with that in mind, there are a few things we have to clear up about what happens in this house and your role in it."

Visitation at My Father's House

Somehow the guilt given to most fathers of divorce passed by my father. I visited my father after my parents' divorce. He lived in Munich and was very German, but funny. He was a loving and strict disciplinarian. He felt that it was his job to teach me the ways of the world, according to him. That he did. He did it with tasks, order, and my expected compliance because he was my father and he was teaching me, sometimes sternly, most times with humor and love. When I visited his home I was treated as one of the family—which meant I had tasks, duties, manners, and a dress code to abide by. It was the sixties, and my idea of getting dressed was a clean pair of blue jeans and a clean shirt. My father would have none of that. He'd say, "When we have dinner in this house, you will wear a skirt. You will comb your hair and live by the rules of this household." These were things I had to do, much as they were against my very principles at the time. And I did them.

At my father's home we often had guests for dinner who spoke Bavarian. My father insisted that I learn the dialect as a courteous gesture to our visitors. It seemed like an outrageous request to me; our family was from the north, where the "best" German was spoken. Yet there was never any doubt that I would do what was expected. I learned Bavarian.

Ten Rules for Fathers Who Divorce

1. Accept that Guilt Is a Prime Mover in Your Actions. Know that you are not alone in feeling guilty about your divorce. Most men feel guilty because they lost their family and their power as father to that family. You may also feel guilty if you believe the mother of your children is not doing an adequate job of parenting.

2. Make the Most of Your Visitation. On the average, fathers of divorce and remarriage see their children every other weekend, Wednesday nights, alternate holidays, and for a month or two in the summer. The rules of visitation need to be set precisely and specifically. Children need predictability. Dad must arrive on time to pick them up; five o'clock on Friday is not five-thirty. Bringing them back on time is essential, too.

3. The Children at Your House Live by the Rules of Your House. Your children need to become part of your household, not just guests in your home. If you are married or living with a woman, you must confer with her and decide specifically what your expectations as a couple are toward the visiting children. Appropriate behavior and acceptable manners must be decided upon by the couple. Chores must be assigned; making beds, helping with meals, keeping the bathroom clean, etc. Structure equals love. Chaos and unpredictability creates low self-esteem in a child.

4. Don't Be a Wimp Father. Most men—even the strongest and most powerful—wimp out and turn into ninety-pound weaklings when their children visit. They endeavor to be "buddies" to their child. We so often hear fathers saying, "I see them so little; I don't want to waste time being their disciplinarian." This attitude often results in upsetting the wife or female partner as the children get more and more out of control. Remember, discipline means guidance.

5. Create High Self-Esteem in Your Children. This is done by creating predictable expectations for your children when they come to your house. Predictable rules and regulations will make your children feel safe and secure.

6. Money Is Always a Problem, No Matter How Much There Is. It is often best when children visit to give them a specific allowance for the time they will be with you. In return for the money the child receives, he/she is expected to be a good citizen of the household, do chores, and then use the money as he or she sees fit (a good rule of thumb is to give your kid enough money for a trip to the movies, some time at the video arcade, a couple of slices of pizza, etc.). Providing less than what is usual and customary for weekend spending will result in your having to dip into your pocket again anyway. If a child needs extra money, we advocate "extra pay for extra jobs."

7. Build and Maintain Couple Strength. Work together with your partner. Don't argue in front of the children. Discussion is okay, but arguments are not. Be respectful of her reality as well as your own regarding the assignment of chores. Work this out between you, or seek the help of a Stepfamily Foundation counselor. The couple are the two pillars that hold the family together: She is the female head of the household; he is the male head of the household.

8. The Couple Decides the Rules of Discipline. The couple decides the Rules of the House: chores and manners. The biological parent disciplines the child whenever possible. When necessary the stepparent says, "In this house we . . ." in order to avoid the "You're not my mother; you can't tell me what to do" syndrome.

9. Creating a Structure Is Vital for the Children. This requires extending the Rules of the House to all events, such as a system for helping with the dishes, yard work, making your bed, keeping your room in order, and helping adults. This structure makes it easy for kids to know what to do at your house. It doesn't matter that the rules are different than Mom's. Creating a structure means creating high self-esteem. Children like themselves better when they know that they have done a good job and are part of a team.

10. Remember that You Are the Father and the Male Head of the Household. Men teach children the ways of the still dominant, male hierarchical business structure.

The Stepfather: Common Complaints

- Here she was alone with those kids, I come in to put some order in the place . . . and they all reject me.
- I can't teach them what they need to learn from a man. She doesn't support me.
- She always jumps to the kids' defense when I correct them. She's turning her boys into wimps.
- She says I'm too tough. Kids who misbehave need someone to be tough with them.
- I give her kids the gift of my time and no one says thank you.
- They're fresh, don't help her, and never, unless I raise my voice, listen to me.
- A man has to be King of his Castle. I feel like the houseboy.
- It's her house, the kids were there before me, and they let me know that.
- My wife treats me like an outsider when it comes to the kids.
- They need a man around here, and she and they won't let me be one!
- I buy the kids stuff and they hardly say thank you.
- She has been too busy with her job to be a mother.
- There is so much tension in the house when the children are here.
- I love her so much when we're alone and they're at their father's house.
- People write about the plight of the stepmother. What about the stepfather?
- Who acknowledges what I'm really feeling—emasculated in my own home.
- I feel like a third wheel when I'm with her and her kids.
- I'm not the head of this house; the kids run it and she lets them.
- I must come first for this to work.

We don't often hear about the stepfather. There has been no trace of him in fairy tales, myths, or legends. Although today we will occasionally see him in a made-for-TV movie—usually as a child abuser or sexual molester—he is close to nonexistent in our collective imagination.

I suspect that gap won't be filled readily, as fewer and fewer men are now willing to marry women with children. Although I have no statistical evidence to support that, I make the observation on what I have seen in my practice.

Still, within at least some small circles, the stepfather is beginning to be recognized as a potentially significant figure in his new household who can have a very real impact on his stepkids: positive and negative.

Regrettably, it's often the latter. And the marriage also suffers dreadfully. On more than one occasion, a stepfather in counseling has remarked, "I wish the kids would go play in traffic." He's only half kidding. These feelings don't escape the kids or the mother, who now feels even more defensive and protective of her children. Hostility can become the name of the game.

Like everyone else, the stepfather comes to his new household with a host of unrealistic expectations, including the biggie: "I'm the boss!" He frequently comes on too hard, too soon and, not surprisingly, within short order the kids rebel and everyone feels disappointed and resentful. The end result may be that the stepfather withdraws altogether, psychologically and perhaps literally.

And all of the unhappiness may be compounded by the ever-present money conflicts—in some instances the stepfather is supporting two households—and the gnawing feeling, on his part, that he has abandoned his *own* children, if he has any. After all, they're now being raised by a mom he divorced and maybe her new husband, whom he may not like much either.

The good news is that if all of these issues are recognized and dealt with intelligently, a lot of the problems can be mitigated; indeed, transformed into good relationships and experiences.

Let's start with the most obvious:

The male has generally been accustomed to being the head of the household and may enter into this new household expecting to mold his new stepfamily into his idea of a well-behaved, respectful, orderly family. "Now that I'm a part of this household, we'll start doing things properly. . . . Beds will be made, dishes will be done, doors will not be slammed, and appropriate language will be used. . . ."

Most often the stepfather steps into a situation where there is already an established way of doing things. And the truth is that working single mothers often fall behind on discipline. Stepfathers may complain that their wives overindulge and underparent their children. The children and mothers have relationships that have lasted their entire lives, while the couples' relationships are relatively new.

Mom says, "You can't treat my children that way. They're going through a difficult time." The kids say, "You're not my father, I don't have to do what you tell me." When new order is imposed distress runs high on all sides.

And then the heavy-duty destructive eruptions begin. He says, "Your kids run this household. You don't teach them manners. They'll never be anything when they grow up." She says, "How dare you talk to me that way? You act like the children are annoying you all the time. You wish they weren't here."

It is important to realize that the problems aren't caused by the individuals, but by the very situation of step. The stepfamily does not function like an intact family. In a biological family if I do *A,* then the result will be *B.* In a stepfamily, if I do *A,* the result will be *M.* We need to learn to accept that there are different realities in step.

There is my reality and your reality, and in the household we must create a merger between the two, always maintaining respect for both.

In intact families, children are masters at splitting the parents.

If one says "no" they ask the other, and a mini problem may develop. In stepfamilies the mini problem can quickly become a maxi problem. If Mom says "yes" and Stepdad says "no," she may be doubly upset with Stepdad precisely because he is the outsider and can't possibly have the attachment to her children that she has.

It is important to be in agreement when dealing with the children. The couple must sit down together and decide how they are going to run their household. The couple must draw up guidelines, operating procedures, rules of conduct, and job descriptions for everyone in the household. Often we need to seek the help of a trained stepfamily counselor to work out impasses. Impasses between the couple can erode couple strength, which is the very foundation of the stepfamily.

Many solutions can be found if the problems are approached from a managerial perspective. Meetings between husband and wife, mother and son, stepfather and stepdaughter, must be scheduled and written down as appointments.

The Stepfather as a Special Resource

Remember, in step the good news is that you get more. Stepfathers should think of themselves as resource people for their stepchildren and take the opportunity to spend some time alone with them: throw a ball, catch a fish, take them to the office, and work together instead of separately on household chores.

Express interest in their interests. If your stepdaughters enjoy ballet, buy them a book on ballet or take them to the ballet. Their mother doesn't have to be included. Similarly, if your stepson is turned on to science, join him on a trip to the local science museum or teach him what you know about astronomy. Share *your* interests with your stepchildren. Who knows? They might become theirs, too.

Remember that the children are traumatized and may still be going through a grieving process for their old family. You are an alien in this house. You have different blood and a different background. It takes time, energy, and work. But the rewards may be grateful and devoted children in your life.

And there's an additional bonus: Paying special attention to your stepchildren will endear you to the woman in your life.

The Stepfather as Male Role Model

The stepfather can have a special place in the life of his stepson. And this is particularly important in a relationship that may already be defined by strong, deep-seated antagonisms that are not uncommon in same sex step relations. Not to overstate the case, but Oedipal feelings are alive and well.

On a more superficial level—and perhaps it's not all that superficial—there may be other sources of conflict between stepfather and stepson, especially if the boy lived a long time with a single mother before the stepfather came into the picture. He could be overprotected and perhaps even sissyish. This is a big turn-off to a lot of new stepdads. But consider it from the kid's point of view: How would he possibly know the ways of men in a male world? Who taught him?

And that's where you come in—enter the stepfather: teacher, buddy, and fellow man.

I vividly remember the wonderful relationship that developed between my son Lars (from a former marriage) and my second husband, Bob. It didn't happen immediately, but ultimately there was a lovely bonding between the two of them.

An early episode: Lars was all of ten when Bob noticed, "He doesn't know how to shake hands like a man." I was very upset. I said, "What can I do?" Bob responded, "Let me teach him." Turning to Lars, he instructed, "Look me in the eye, grip my hand firmly, and shake." They practiced it several times until Lars got it right. When he did Bob congratulated him, and Lars beamed with pleasure.

It was a detail, but not without significance, that paved the way for the next ten years of their relationship. Throughout that time Bob always made a point of engaging Lars in many activities that frequently excluded me. And, yes, I encouraged it—I felt the male bonding was that important, even if that meant playing, on occasion, female-who-was-not-up-to-the-task. The point is, it was so good to see them going off together *as men*—to fish, to ski, whatever—I was only too happy to be relegated to the role of woman as outsider. I can still hear them laughing, as they gestured at me, "Oh, she's a woman; she can't do it."

What's revealing—striking—to me is that to this day Lars, who is now thirty-one, sounds and walks like his stepfather Bob. Watching Lars from the back, I sometimes do a double take, he resembles Bob so much.

My Stepfather

I, too, was lucky in my relationship with my stepfather, a loving man who consistently handled conflicts with grace and calm purposefulness.

Consider this episode—it's about my testing boundaries and acting out—and how beautifully my stepfather handled it. The memory continues to have resonance for me thirty years down the road.

I was a twenty-five-year-old married woman and TV reporter at the time. On weekends I would go out to visit my mother and stepfather at their beautiful home in Old Westbury, New York. My stepfather had a wonderful lawn. He mowed it himself, using a small tractor on which he sat and carefully tended his beloved grass.

Across the way from the house was a small racetrack where I used to exercise racehorses. I had trained animals all my life, and working with the young racehorses was my passion and relaxation.

One day, and for no apparent reason, I decided to take the lead pony and ride him over to the house and gallop him around my stepfather's lawn. My mother was taking her customary afternoon nap. Three times I galloped hard around that lawn, in and out of and between my stepfather's favorite oak trees. No one came out. I put the horse back and returned home. If I had done something like this to my father—and I never would have—he would have had my head. I had, in fact, created great hoofprints on the soft spring lawn, thus almost destroying a great source of pride for my stepfather.

As I walked home, all seemed quiet. Then I saw my stepfather, Russell, standing on the driveway near the house. He didn't appear angry. He said, "Jeannette, it will take me the whole weekend to pound out those hoofprints." And he said nothing more. I looked at him and began to cry. Together, that evening and the next day, we pounded out the hoofprints, and we worked the day after that, as well.

Somehow, after that, I knew I could trust this man. My mother never said a thing. To this day, I don't know why I did it. But from that day on our relationship was solid. Even thinking about him standing there—not angry but saddened, dear, loving, caring—brings tears to my eyes. Russell is gone, but his compassion lives on.

Ten Rules for Stepfathers

1. The Stepfather Can't Function as Does the Biological Father. He is not the father and never will be. The stepfather is the male head of the household. Together with his wife, the children's mother, he can be a guide, a mentor, and even a psychological father to the stepchildren, over time. Go slow.

2. Structuring the Household Is a Shared Task Between Husband and Wife. How is the time, energy, and money used? What are the duties, responsibilities, and contributions of each member of the household? This must be sorted out and decided by the couple.

3. The Norms and Forms of Discipline Must Be Discussed and Agreed to by the Couple. Generally, the biological parent does the disciplining and the stepparent reminds, "In this house we . . ."

4. "Overdisciplining Your Stepchildren"—Watch It! The biological mother can perceive it as too much, too often. This can bring on the mama-bear-protecting-her-young-from-the-outsider syndrome.

5. "Underdisciplining Your Own Children"—Watch It! The biological father without custody misses his kids and fears the loss of affection and his personal input to his children. This is a legitimate fear. The less time he has with them, the less he wants to discipline. Children need parents—even visiting parents—to set up predictable structures and limits. Set up the rules quickly so you spend less time disciplining.

6. Predictability and Organization Create Intimacy. In a home with structure parents and children spend less time negotiating and arguing. Parent/child power struggles over repetitive issues waste time and undermine the child's self-esteem. Talking about real issues and creating intimacy should be the goal during these limited times together.

7. If Things Don't Work, the Tendency Is to Withdraw. Don't. Stepfathering is complicated, and the notion of not being the "master" of your own household is tough. Indeed, the mother may be lax on discipline. Indeed, you want to change things. Stepfathering has to do with parenting. You and the mother must, together, work out the forms and norms.

8. Unrealistic Expectations Beget Rejections and Resentments. There are few models for stepfathers. Learn the dynamics of step and divorce. Know what to expect and what not to expect.

9. Be Aware of a Conflict between Sexual and Biological Pulls in Stepfamily Relationships. In the original family the couple comes together to have a child, and together their energies focus on that child. The child is an extension of themselves. In step the child is connected to only one person in the couple. The blood ties and sexual ties can be polarized and can pull the couple in opposite directions.

10. Guard Your Sense of Humor and Use It.

Women in Step: The Divorced Mother of the Children

It's difficult to have a good relationship with one's ex, especially for the ex-wife, who may be angry and hurt. She may feel that she has the daily burdens of child-rearing while he takes the kids on great vacations. Then there are the money issues. The fact is that many divorced women's standard of living plummets while their ex's continues to rise. And because she is still angry at him, she may even feel, "The kids deserve to know how awful he is." Without meaning to, she is hurting them and their self-esteem. No matter how bad Pop is, he is still half of them. The point is, should they think ill of their father, they will, unconsciously and/or consciously, think badly of themselves.

The Single Mother with Custody: Classic Complaints

- I have all the daily burdens and then he gets the kids every other weekend and takes them on great vacations with his girlfriend.
- I feel that I have too much responsibility with not enough money to handle it.
- When the kids visit him he plays with them. He is the classic Disneyland Daddy.
- The kids love it. They're treated like princes and princesses. They never have to help.
- My living standard has plummeted as his continues to increase.
- The children are my responsibility. He does so little to discipline or guide them.
- His payments are late, yet he expects me to have the kids well dressed and on time when he wants them.
- Why shouldn't I bad-mouth him to the kids? They deserve to know how awful he is.
- I hardly have time to date, and who wants a woman with kids?
- He married this young thing and the kids say they can't stand her.
- Who is she to tell my children what to do?
- I told the children that they don't have to listen to her, or obey her.
- The kids tell me everything that happens at that house.
- I think he and the new wife fight a lot over the children.
- I would never talk to her.
- He hasn't got a good word to say about all those years I raised our children.
- We have very little contact. He picks them up and honks the horn.

Dangers for the Single Mother

The mother after divorce can still be angry at her ex, the children's father. She is a mother alone. She may feel vengeful. Remember Shakespeare's famous words, "Hell hath no fury like a woman scorned."

"Bad-mouthing"

Because she is still angry at her ex, she may "bad-mouth" him or give him a "rough time." The danger is that without meaning to, she will hurt her own children. Should they feel bad about him, their father, they will also feel bad about themselves. No matter how bad he is, it is best for the mother not to bad-mouth the children's father. The result will be lack of self-esteem in the children.

Time

Should she seek to find another man or husband, she may take time away from her children. Should she focus on her children and not date, she has little personal life except for the children.

Discipline—Guiding and Parenting

She, too, may work and find little time to discipline. Just like the wimp father, she too may become the wimp mother. Too tired to guide, to teach the things mothers teach, she finds herself not disciplining, letting things go, and not even planning meals with the children. TV takes over the parenting. Dining becomes feeding the kids, work pays the bills, the children become "latchkey kids." And here we see the loss of the most important place for all of us, the home and family.

Ten Steps for the Single Mother with Custody

1. There Are No Ex Parents, Only Ex Spouses! Co-parenting is good for children. See a counselor. Work on talking to each other, respectfully, as parents of your children. We want emotional well-being for our children. Having two biological parents who can positively relate, even if only over the children, does important things for the kids' self-esteem.

2. Don't "Bad-Mouth" Your Ex, Their Father. The result is lowered self-esteem in the child. That child is half of both of you, so when we say bad things about your ex, no matter how true, this damages the child's self-worth.

3. Don't Share Your Hurts and Bad Feelings with the Kids. Find a peer. When we share our hurts with children, and they can do nothing about them, we lessen their feeling of self-worth or make them feel like they are running the show.

4. Be the Female Head of Your Household. Rules, chores, manners, and respect for your position as mother is vital for their sense of how the world works and vital for their taking their position in the world later. They must learn the hierarchy is headed by you, not them.

5. If at All Possible, Communicate with His New Woman. You may find you have a lot to talk about. Also, it helps the children to see you two cooperating, rather than hating each other. It *is* hard. It takes forgiveness and grace . . . and it's good for the children.

6. Money Is never Enough, nor Is It Used Properly for Everyone. And, oh how he spends it on the kids! Your standard of living has dropped while his has increased.

7. If You Are Dating, Be Careful not to Make Him More Important than Your Children. They will sense something vital and exciting happening to you when you rush to get dressed and make a fuss over him. They lost one parent and often fear losing the other. So go slow. Don't make it a big deal, and present him as a "friend" until there might be something serious.

8. Don't Show Sexual Activity. Not even evidence of it, until the relationship is serious. Children pick up your attachment and the energy of sexuality. They may make life very difficult for your lover because they fear they will lose you.

9. When that Adolescent Boy Becomes Too Hard to Handle. As hard as it is, it may be time for his father to have custody, if he knows how to guide and discipline effectively.

10. Keep Your Sense of Humor and Your Belief in a Higher Power. You will need both.

The Stepmother's Common Complaints

• Everyone in his life, his kids, his former wife, and his business, comes before me.

• He expects me to treat them as if I were their own mother.

• I want a child of my own, and he's had enough.

• His ex calls and he jumps to her commands. It seems as though she has more influence on him than anybody. My money goes to support this family because his money goes to take care of her and them.

• His former wife never says thank you for any of the things I do.

• The children treat me like the maid; I'm expected to do everything that their mother would do for them. Even the cleaning lady gets more appreciation than I do.

• He believes that buying them something, or entertaining, is fathering.

• Guilt runs his relationship with the children.

• I think I'm becoming the "cruel" stepmother.

• The worst of it is, when his children come over we have no sex life.

- So he expects me to be kind to them, cook for them, and accompany them on outings with him, and then when we go to bed he is too guilty or "wimped out" to make love to me. And he wonders why I'm bitchy.
- All these kids seem to be able to say is, "Do me, buy me, and drive me."
- We disagree completely on discipline.
- I work hard all week, and then he and they expect me to be there for them on the weekends.
- Sometimes he expects me to be there and handle his children while he's in the office or off playing golf.
- *I want to come first* in his life.

Jack and Janice

She simply didn't understand it. Janice had been so close to Jack's children before they were married: long conversations, intimacies exchanged, laughter and giggles. Jack had said many times, "You're marvelous with my girls. They tell you far more than they've ever told me."

Then, at the wedding, Babs had cried. Janice had thought it was because of the beauty of the ceremony; she and Jack had written it themselves. Even before hugging her son Andy, she'd gone running over to the girls to hug them and kiss them, saying, "Now I have the daughters I've always wanted." They pulled back.

That was the beginning. Marriage, tender love, long delightful nights of conversation and warmth. Then Sunday would come. Jack's three girls would come and stay for dinner. The wonderful big family gatherings that Janice had dreamed about didn't happen.

Andy was so excited at the prospect of being part of a large family that he'd overact, overdo everything. When he wasn't noticed, he'd go from unruliness to whining. Often, after a few reprimands from Jack, he'd slink off to his room and watch television alone.

From the first, things seemed to go wrong. The girls were distant and cool. Her efforts at conversation were responded to in monosyllables. They hid behind magazines and newspapers. It was as though they didn't even want to look at Janice or Andy.

One of those early Sundays she really blew it. First she insisted they say hello to Andy. Then she asked them to help her serve the dinner. Jack said they didn't have to help. She served the dinner alone, feeling like a servant. Before she even got all the plates on the table, heads were bent over, slurping up food. Some were practically finished before she sat down. Nobody looked at her, and nobody said anything to Andy.

"That's it!" She slammed her fist on the table. "Couldn't you at least have waited until we were all served?"

"That's the way we do it," Jack said. "The food will get cold, and besides, they're hungry."

Janice couldn't help it. She started a total tirade about the difference between dining and eating. She suggested that next time they put their plates on the floor and eat with the dog.

Carefully, the girls stared at their plates and forcefully moved the food into their mouths. Fork to mouth. Fork to plate. And back again. Arms working like pistons. As soon as they could, they left. Linda slammed the door.

Janice and Jack had a free-for-all attacking each other's children. Why had he defended them and not her? Why had she jumped on them? They hadn't done anything wrong. Didn't she have the perception to tell they were shy? And her sissy son, with his weird noises. Wouldn't he ever stop whining? His stupid daughters showed no breeding whatsoever. Why did she keep babying that kid of hers? You and yours. No, yours and you. Uproar. Then silence and separateness. What was happening to their love?

This scenario is all too common. It's dreadful for everyone, but especially the stepmother. Traditionally, indeed for eons, the female ran the home. In the house she had the responsibility to teach manners, duties, how meals were eaten and served. Her husband backed her up with the children and deferred to her in the domain of the house.

No more! That age-old ideal is even rare for biological mothers in intact families. But the stepmother has two strikes against her . . . just for openers.

For starters, she is *not* the biological mother; thus her central role in the family is rendered meaningless. Secondly, she often works. While the biological mother may also be balancing work and family, the stepmother faces her stepmothering duties, new couple demands, *and* the pulls of her job.

And the fact that she is rarely thanked doesn't help. Even if Dad attempts to elicit some expressions of gratitude from the kids, they usually balk. "Gratitude?" the kids respond. "Who wants her anyway?" Not only does she not come first in the eyes of her husband, but the children resent her. Ironically, they might love her if she were an aunt or friend of the family, but as a stepmother they despise her.

Stepmothers were never born with "cruel" on their passport, but it's easy to become that way, given the dynamics of step relationships. She asks her husband to defend her in front of the children; he doesn't. She comments on their bad manners, how rudely they talk to him (and her), and the fact that they don't help her around the house; he finds nothing wrong with it. And then there's the amount of time he gives them at her expense. All during his single-dad days, he had spent his time tending to their bedtime, delaying it, reading stories until late. Now that he's a married man, he's still up there with his children, forever it seems. She sits in the living room, alone . . . waiting, waiting, and waiting. In short, she has lost her role as a woman, as female head of the house, and feels she comes a distant second to the kids.

In many ways the stepmother's plight is similar to the stepfather's. They are both outsiders who seek to establish themselves as a pillar of the household alongside their partners.

What Is the Stepmother's Role?

She is the female head of the household. She is never the "mother." Even if the mother is dead, the word "mother" is a holy one. For the child there is no replacing the mother, *especially* if she is dead.

So the stepmother's position is a delicate one. She is the substitute. She is there, "where my mom is supposed to be." She is treated by the children much like the substitute teacher at school . . . badly. This phenomenon holds true for the stepfather also.

The stepmother must decide, together with her mate, just what are the "rules of this house." This is to be done out of earshot of the kids, and perhaps with the help of a therapist. Dad will bring some forms and norms, some ways of disciplining, some expectations as to duties, chores, and responsibilities, and so will Stepmom. These must be worked out *together* and then presented to the children. The children have a vote, but no veto as to the rules.

And in the same way that it takes the stepfather time to endear himself to his stepkids, it also takes the stepmother time, energy, and effort. But as long as she remembers—just like the stepdad—that she has something special to offer the kids, the first rung of the ladder has been climbed. I recall my stepdaughters telling me they could talk to me about certain subjects, such as boys and sex, that they would never dream of discussing with their mother, let alone their father.

But that didn't happen overnight. The ice had to be broken. And I, as the adult, had to make the first move.

During my first marriage and before my second marriage, I'd worked as a journalist for twelve years. Now through my fairy godmother I was miraculously transformed into a non-working, they-lived-happily-ever-after wife, mother, and stepmother. I found that being a full-time working mother was nowhere as difficult as being a part-time stepmother.

I remember those first few weekends of our marriage, the days Bob's girls would come to stay. Even now I feel it in my stomach. For thirty-odd years I'd lived with a cast-iron stomach. Nothing upset it, not even cotton candy, hot dogs, roller coasters, or small planes in hurricanes. Nothing, but nothing, bothered my stomach.

Early Saturday mornings I'd begin to feel sick, like I was pregnant or something. I was pregnant, all right—with fear and a heavy implantation of resentment.

They would come in and hardly say hello. I would reach out to them; they would walk away. I would speak; they would say little or nothing. They got me where it hurt the worst. The more I talked, the less they responded.

I simply wasn't aware at the time that these girls had suffered a severe loss when Bob and I became husband and wife. They could never lose their father, but in actual time and attention they had indeed lost a good part of him—to me. Without wanting it or knowing it, we were catapulted into a game of emotional Capture the Flag, and the prize was Bob. To whom would he show loyalty? With whom would he side?

Lucky girls, to be getting me—and Lars, the little brother I knew they had always wanted. Not as far as they were concerned. I was something they had to put up with in order to see their father. Now I wasn't Jeannette, the fun friend; I was Jeannette, the usurper of their father. Neither they nor I could articulate these feelings at the time, but they let me have it: the brunt of their emotions, without even an explanatory note.

And their father, my love, my prince charming, the man for whom I had thrown away my television-reporter status—what did he do? Nothing. They attacked me, and he quietly listened as they tore every feather from my crown. They were impolite, rude, and emotionally crude. Should I defend myself, he would take *their* side. For the first time in my life I was tongue-tied. Disbelieving what was going on, I sat stymied, too afraid to speak. Should I let that anger out, it would surely disembowel our new marriage.

Once, after they had left, I attempted to talk with my husband about it. I struck out. I got nowhere in the battle of my children/ your children. They were no problem, he said; I was the problem. For the first time in my adult life I really felt helpless. What had I gotten myself into? I'd rather interview the president, cover a plane crash, have seventeen for dinner, than spend those lonely days trying to figure out how I could manage this job of mother, stepmother, and wife.

Well, it took about three weeks. I typed memos in quadruplicate, tore them up, and finally picked up the telephone. I asked the two oldest to come up to the house one weekday after school. I wanted to talk to them alone, without their dad. They came. I was determined not to fire off my anger at them, but to get them to understand where I was at.

It was probably the wisest move I ever made on the level of interpersonal relationships.

They walked in the door with their eyes cast on the floor, as though there was something about to be found there. I said little, none of the usual, "How are you? What's happening at school," etc. I allowed moments to pass, no longer rushing. It was my time to say my piece. I began slowly.

"I know it's a difficult time for you children . . . problems between your father and your mother. It's hard having your dad's new wife around, and your mom's new husband. I'll bet you feel left out a lot. I feel left out a lot myself. I'm aware that there are problems for you—but there are problems for me, too."

I made it very clear that I had no intention of taking their father from them, that the house was always open to them. I explained that I perceived their behavior as lack of interest in me and my son, as rudeness. That I felt offended. "For example, when you call, you just ask, 'Is Dad there?' No 'Hi, Jeannette, how are you?'

You've used the only weapon I can't deal with," I told them, "and that is your back. You've turned your back on me, ignored me, walked away from me. It hurts.

"Never once since the marriage have you asked me about me or mine or what I was doing. It's always been me doing the work, talking to you, and trying to discover what you were doing and feeling.

"I've got to tell you right now, one human being to another, that I'm very angry about it.

"I offer you a new start. We can sit here; we can talk. Or we can use your favorite weapon and turn our backs on each other. I say the choice is yours."

Silence. The beautiful blond-haired second oldest began to cry quietly. Then the oldest said, "Yes, it's difficult for us. We're just not good at communicating. Even some of our friends tell us we're hard to talk to. . . ."

I had brought them both to tears, or perhaps just allowed their tears. I moved over uneasily and sat between them. We hugged each other like children. To this day I don't remember whether I cried or not. We all had a lot to cry about. But now at least it was there in front of us.

This one episode did *not* bring the whole story to a happy ending. But it was a step to openness and acceptance of our feelings—and a clear delineation of what I couldn't and wouldn't take from them.

Ten Rules for Stepmothers

1. Know the Natural Dynamics and Behaviors of Step. Don't blame yourself. Recognize that the kids are acting out their grief at the loss of the family, no matter how long ago it was. They will also constantly test the strength of the couple.

2. Super-Stepparenting Doesn't Work. Go Slow.

3. The Couple Decides on the Rules of the House. Discipline, chores, manners, and meals must be worked out as a partnership or they will not work.

4. Don't Discipline If You and He Haven't Agreed on Forms, Norms, and Structure.

5. Build Couple Strength by working on and agreeing on structure and discipline together, or with a Stepfamily Foundation–trained therapist.

6. The Biological Parent Disciplines, Whenever Possible. The stepmother reminds, "Your dad and I have decided that . . ."

7. Hold Family Meetings. Write down the rules of the house. The biological parent presents them. The kids have a vote, but no veto. Post the "Rules of this House" on the refrigerator. Believe it or not, kids like having rules and like showing them to their friends. There must be positive and negative consequences.

8. Take Time Out for Yourselves as a Couple. "Date night" is highly recommended.

9. Fathers Often Fear the Loss of the Children If They Discipline. It's common for the divorced father to be oblivious to bad behavior. This is not fathering. This is not your place to tell him. He usually thinks you're just too tough. Get expert advice for him to read or talk to.

10. Take Time for Yourself when he has visitation. You don't have to be there all the time. These are not your kids. You don't have to love them, but they must respect your position as female head of the household, as told to them by their father. You'll need your sense of humor and a belief in a Higher Power. Don't lose it!

Chapter 3

THE REALITIES OF STEP

A stepfamily isn't a biological family, and trying to make it run like one just won't work. Yet, every day hopeful people try to force their stepfamilies to act, look, and work like a biological family. They soon find themselves disappointed, disillusioned, and divorced.

Let's look at some of the realities of step.

To say "We are a family, not a *step*family" may feel good at the outset. But the reality is that you *are* a stepfamily. "Step" isn't a dirty word to be avoided when describing your family situation. It's a descriptive term that identifies the relationship of one family member to another. Your stepchild is not your biological child; she is your spouse's child and your stepchild. You can refer to her as your spouse's child or as your stepchild with equal accuracy and grace.

You aren't the child's "father" or "mother." You're the *step*father or *step*mother. Don't shy away from the terms. A large part of the problem lies in the myths and misunderstandings that surround step relationships.

Some of the realities of the stepfamily that many people try to ignore, and that don't go away, are discussed in this chapter. In the chapters that follow, you'll learn to deal with these realities and to make them work for your step relationship.

1. Stepfamilies are different from biological families—not better or worse, just different. They function according to a different paradigm of the family and a different set of dynamics and behaviors.

Distaste for the word "stepfamily" and the desire to make the stepfamily mimic the biological family creates a wide range of false expectations. They also lead to a denial of the many adjustments that the members of the stepfamily must make. The way to overcome problems is to identify them, most of the problems in step situations are due to the failure of stepfamily members to acknowledge that the step situation does, indeed, create a special need for education and understanding.

An important difficulty in step is finding agreed-upon roles for all family members. Specific rights and responsibilities fall to the male parent, the female parent, and each of the children, according to sex and birth order. When a stepfamily is formed, all the rules change, and the players often shift in their roles.

People entering step are often surprised to find that they have to create new models, new responsibilities, and new job descriptions for each family member. They don't realize at first that a whole new set of step manners is needed. Instead of family relationships that develop naturally, stepfamily relationships require that a new system be created and enforced by the male and female heads of the household. Each step system becomes a new team with new strategies, new positions, and a new team spirit. Actions and behaviors can't be left to chance, but must be spelled out by the couple so that all of the members know their roles.

There are many differences between intact and stepfamilies, some more important than others. Very little in a stepfamily can be taken for granted. When "Mom" or "Dad" does something nice for the kids, it's just taken for granted as being part of the parenting role. But stepparents need to be thanked for what the parent does naturally and without acknowledgment. The parent can easily view his child as an extension of himself. As a result, tasks performed for biological children come more easily to the biological parent than to the stepparent. This doesn't mean that stepparents are cruel or indifferent. Being selfless is simply more difficult with a stepchild than with one's own child.

Children may find "thank you" to be alien to their vocabulary unless they are taught otherwise. When the stepparent performs tasks that are naturally handled by the biological parent, the child is even less likely to say "thank you." It's important to make thank yous a vital part of your new family "language." It's one of the simplest and most basic changes you will have to establish—and it will pave the way for a constructive attitude toward the step situation.

2. You won't be one big happy family at the outset. Don't expect "instant love." Mutual respect is the key.

Individuals in every family may resent each other and try to ignore each other's existence. These rejections are a normal facet of family life. When such rejection occurs in the stepfamily, however, sparks may fly and resentments may burn.

In most cases, biological parents and children will accept and explain away a wide range of behaviors because they are related. They defend, both consciously and unconsciously, behavior that would astound outsiders. Such defenses rest on years and even lifetimes of living together and growing to understand each other. Stepfamily members have no such ties.

Mothers and fathers want to love and nurture their children and often place the needs of their children above their own. In a biologically connected family, the children are an extension of their parents, who naturally want to devote time, energy, and money to them. For the stepperson, no blood bonds exist. Instead of finding his or her behavior easily accepted, the stepfamily member may encounter what seems like unfair criticism. In contrast to the pride and the loving feelings of the natural parent, the stepparent may wish the children didn't exist at all. Hence the fairy tales depicting cruel stepparents and stepchildren.

When two families are joined in a step situation it is easy to expect that everybody involved will share the love of the two spouses. "Of course I will love your child, and she will love me, because you and I love each other." But how can we expect this so blithely? Especially when the myth is forced on everyone in the step situation, you're in for resistance and resentment.

There is no such thing as "instant love" in a stepfamily. While in other areas of life we may simply fall into love, love in step is usually a hard-won victory. The Brady Bunch, alas, is only a sitcom. Love and familial feeling may be encouraged as soon as you enter a step relationship, even at the dating stage. Once you're married the work gets tougher.

The stepfamily does not have years to grow around each other and with each other, like a biological family. Instead, a working team must be *created*—and quickly. The couple has to decide up front how duties, responsibilities, manners, discipline, money, inheritances, and other aspects of life are to be handled.

In step, only a very few big, happy families evolve *naturally*. It's up to you and your spouse to take the lead in setting the family guidelines and in declaring firmly what you will and will not allow in your household. Creating the rules and enforcing them means that you also have to develop couple strength. Couple strength is important to your marriage, of course, but it is vital to the stability of your stepfamily. You will find that many of your decisions will be unpopular—even bitterly resented. But as long as you and your spouse are united in mutual love and respect, *your family will weather the storm.*

3. Stepparenting can be hazardous to your sex life.

Acquiring an instant family, complete with children, can seriously hamper sexual spontaneity. In any marriage, adjusting to each other's idiosyncrasies is an enormous challenge. But with the additional adjustment to children, what chance does your sex life have? The answer is: plenty—as long as you're prepared for the problem!

In the biological family, children usually enter the picture after the couple has had months or years alone. Routines are established, individual habits are known, and bonds are strong between the two adults. When a child is born, the rhythms of the couple and the routine of the household may shift, but place is made for this new being who becomes a *part* of an already established scene. The biological child has the advantage over the stepchild because it is a part of *both* parents. Both parents have created the child, and they tend to dote on any and all of the child's accomplishments as extensions of their own achievements.

When a parent dies or parents divorce, the child and the custodial parent establish routines, habits, and bonds in their life together. When a new spouse and additional children intrude upon this relationship, as they do when the parent remarries and a step relationship is created, a revolution occurs. Many biological parents expect their new mates to adore their children and to understand about the time that must be devoted to them. Similarly, they blithely assume that their children will contentedly accept the newcomer in their lives—even welcome sharing Mommy or Daddy with that newcomer. Unfortunately for us all, it doesn't happen this way.

The reality is that stepparents are less likely to dote upon their stepchildren than are biological parents. In fact, they may feel resentful of the devotion and attention that the biological parent gives to the child. Jealousy and resentment are certainly not exclusive to stepfamilies. They can occur in any family when a new member is added through birth, adoption, or other means.

It's natural for you or your partner to want to come first in the other's life. This happens automatically in first marriages. And in a second marriage, even when the stepparent is fully aware of the needs of the children, the same desire to come first exists. The children, in turn, become confused about their position in this new arrangement. When their parent was single, the children may have come first and may have shared substantially in decision-making and responsibilities. But now that a new adult is seeking to enter the closed circle of the biological parent and child, an adult, moreover, who expects to come first, the child resents it. The child resents having to share his or her parent's love, attention, energy, and money with a person who is still a stranger.

It's a threatening situation for everyone involved. The key to dealing with the tug-of-war between parenting and romance is to set priorities, to organize, and to face facts. Talk over with your partner the demands that a child makes both on you and on the relationship. The step relationship is not one of just romance, but also involves parenting and stepparenting. That reality must be squarely faced and accepted.

The child has to give a little in this situation. Let the child know that he or she is loved very much and no one is going to take that away. Let him/her know equally clearly, however, that he or she is no longer the center of the family's universe—that the family now includes a new member who isn't going to go away. And that, as much as you love the child, you also love your new partner and you want your child to respect that.

4. Everyone will want your attention and time and all at the same moment.

Who do you answer first when your mate and your child call? When your stepchild calls at the same time as your mate? This situation can be ripe for conflict. You can scream for mercy—or, you can take the approach that you only have two ears and one mind.

And remind all stepfamily members that families have long had ranks of importance that are traditionally based on age. Although your child may have come first while you two were on your own, the dynamics of the situation change once the step relationship is established. Children now have to defer to the new male or female household head, and maybe even relocate within the ranks of other children brought into the marriage. This isn't favoritism but survival. It is making order out of chaos.

Certainly, the conflict in responding to family members is not the only loyalty issue in the stepfamily. Children often feel tremendously guilty toward the stepparent. When a child begins to care about the stepparent, he or she may begin misbehaving and act more as if he disdains the stepparent. This behavior results from the child's fear that loving the stepparent is somehow a betrayal of the absent biological parent. It goes something like this: "If I love you it means I don't love my real parent—so I won't love you." The child feels compelled to mention Mommy in Daddy's house and to talk about Daddy in Mommy's house.

Adults also feel guilt for their behavior with both their own and their stepchildren. The parent may feel guilty over enjoying a romantic, candlelight dinner while the child eats an early supper alone. The father feels guilty during visitation when his child wants to be alone with him and not with him *and* his new wife.

These feelings are normal. There are a lot of new feelings to work out in a step relationship, and conflicting loyalties is only one. Yet, it may well be the most explosive feeling of all.

5. Blame the step situation, and not the people involved.

One of the greatest mistakes of stepfamilies is blaming themselves for the feelings and difficulties of the step situation. Such blame not only makes you feel helpless, it also keeps you from taking steps to deal with the problems. Blame, guilt, and recrimination only delay finding solutions.

The chapters that follow will give you the tools to solve your own step problems. They will guide you in developing ways of communicating your concerns, fears, annoyances, and other problems that are obstructing a smooth, healthy family life.

Stepchildren are often blamed for family problems, but this is only a red herring that disguises the true source of the problems.

It's not easy being the child in a step relationship. Complicating this, the child may, consciously or unconsciously, derive a sense of power as a child of death or divorce. Naturally, the child wants to defend his or her territory. This behavior can result in real pain for both the biological parent and the stepparent.

While no one will deny that the presence of stepchildren makes the relationship a more difficult and complex one, blaming the children is only denying that you are not powerless. Only you can take the responsibility for the success or failure of your stepfamily. Only you can establish the guidelines—and *guide* the children in becoming part of that relationship. You will learn how to do so as you read on.

6. There are no ex-parents.

How should we deal with the prior spouse? The answer is: very carefully. Like it or not, parents are forever. Although the prior spouse may intrude continually in your efforts to create a new life and may try to run your home and children as well, you must try to understand. The prior spouse is your child's biological parent and the blood ties may be equally matched by emotional ties. While you might resent having someone no longer married to you meddling in your affairs and trying to influence your children against new relationships, remember that *everyone* in the family of divorce suffered a loss. Power, love, contact, whatever the case, the hurts exist on all fronts.

But how do you deal with behavior that endangers your present life? Even when your former husband or wife is inconsiderate or angry, the most powerful thing you can do is to *not* react in the same way. Open lines of communication between the parents are best for your children.

The children are often caught in the crossfire, being made to listen to one parent downgrade the other, hearing Mommy's new husband or Daddy's new wife "bad-mouth" the other parent, and being subjected to quizzing after each visit, can only cause your children pain. The biological bond can never be broken, and children should not be made to feel guilty for maintaining that bond.

You can never become an ex-parent—only an ex-spouse. Divorce ends the legal marital bond, but your child will forever provide an indissoluble link. This link is the "separation triangle." Although ex-spouses no longer relate as husband and wife, they must establish a working relationship for the children's sake. They will need to keep an open line to discuss ideas and events and make decisions that are important to the guidance and parenting of their children.

For the child, there can be no replacement for the biological parent—nor should there be. We can't reconstitute the family. There are no replacement mothers and fathers, and children know this instinctively. The words "mother" and "father" are charged with a reverence that mystifies many stepparents, who wonder at a child's ability almost to worship the biological parent, no matter what that parent has or has not done. Such feelings in children are instinctive and natural. Even more important, you need to respect such feelings. How you handle a child's relationship with his or her parent will influence your own relationship with the child. Chapter 15 gives you the tools to deal effectively with this situation.

7. Unrealistic expectations can cause difficult disappointments.

Often, in the beginning, unrealistic expectations predominate in step relationships. It is just as unrealistic for a child to expect the new stepparent to be either awful or wonderful as it is for a stepfather to assert: "Now *I'm* the father around this house and we will start running things properly." Equally unrealistic is the stepmother who believes that caring and working hard will cure all ills, or that she can remain uninvolved with her husband's kids with impunity.

It just doesn't happen that way.

The danger with such expectations is that we begin to feel

short-changed and resentful. The only safe expectation of step is that you will get more people—but you will get fewer of the ones you like and more of the ones you don't. And that's a very valuable starting point.

It's important to have great expectations. But unrealistic expectations—expectations based on old models—can beget big disappointments. Let's begin with the stepmother. She comes into the situation with a desire to care and to try to please. Superwoman would be hard-pressed to compete with the superstepmother. She works. She's a homemaker. She's a stepmother. Whatever the family appears to need, she is ready to supply.

She has her counterpart, although less frequently, in the superstepfather. He wants to teach and give the children what he feels they have missed. In the process, he comes on too hard, too fast, and too soon.

Both the stepmother and the stepfather with unrealistic expectations may also feel that they can make the step situation less painful by buying the child's affections with gifts and trips. This never works as they think it will, and in the end they are often sorely disappointed.

8. It's important to establish firm rules for discipline and visitation.

Merging two families can easily result in chaos. In their old lives, hopefully, everyone had a specific role, specific responsibilities, and, yes, a specific seat at the dinner table. When people come together in the step relationship, all of this changes—and at a time when intense emotions are often boiling to the surface.

Step is an emotion-charged situation that grows out of loss. Everyone suffers a loss of position and territory, and many who live in step feel that their position is constantly threatened. The most common problem seems to be that just as you have found your seat in the stepfamily, you may find someone else sitting in it.

The desire to be first and the continual vying for position reverberates throughout step. Adults and children both strain to hold on to old labels, which give them feelings of worth—wife, husband, daddy's girl, mommy's boy, the firstborn, the baby. We feel an urgency to establish position and to claim our turf. Everyone appears to be asking the same questions: "Where do I fit in?" "Where do I rank?" "Am I still important?"

In the biological family, a normal pecking order evolves with each birth. Mommy and Daddy are at the top, and the siblings follow. However, when stepfamilies are created, there is no time nor room for evolution. Two children may be of the same age. The prior spouse may have a substantial role in the lives of the children. The gender mix of the family may change radically.

To prevent the chaos that is bound to erupt in so complex a situation, it is your role as an adult in the step relationship to reorder the family. Everyone needs to have his or her special niche, and these rarely emerge naturally in the step situation. To successfully reorder the family, you and your spouse must establish clear job descriptions for everyone in the family. You will learn how to do this in Chapter 6.

Part of the answer is to make everyone's responsibilities clear. Important areas in which guidelines are needed are: how living spaces are kept; how meals and cleanup are handled; and how you treat each other. For example, while in one household it is customary for the members merely to grunt acknowledgments in the morning and barely to notice each other's departures and arrivals, other households make an event of each small act. You need to determine what your family's style will be and enforce your guidelines. You might tell family members, for example: "In this house, we say 'hello,' 'good-bye,' 'please,' and 'thank you.' "

Discipline is another area in the step experience that can't be left to chance. Discipline does not just mean punishment. It is a means of providing guidance and direction. All of us have been raised with different styles of discipline and each of us has a different view of what will work. In step, we must quickly and consciously decide and define how we will order our households. Discipline and structure must strike a fine balance with caring and love. It's the most guilt-driven behavior. See Chapter 8, which provides a valuable guide to this sensitive issue.

The matter of visitation, even though court ordered in many cases, should also be formally arranged and structured by the adults in the stepfamily situation. Visitation is generally upsetting to everyone, and guidelines should be established to make the process easier.

Each time the child goes between homes, the old feelings and fears around the divorce may be reawakened. Adults are also affected by the process. However, as with any difficulty, visitation works best when it is clearly defined, planned, and anticipated. And the responsibility for this lies with the adults in the step situation.

9. Everyone in step must deal with guilt.

Biological parents feel guilty for loving their new spouses. Stepparents feel guilty for loving someone else's children. Children feel guilty for loving a stepparent or a stepsibling.

The absent biological father often feels and exhibits that he never sees his child enough to make a difference. He feels that he failed at the marriage. He hears complaints that his payments are inadequate. He feels that his child is being raised by a woman whom he can no longer influence and for whom he no longer cares. He frequently feels that he only gets the bills and not the blessings of fatherhood.

Most of all, he suffers from the dreaded fear of losing his children, a fear that is not unfounded. The bitter truth is that a great percentage of absent biological parents actually do, for all intents and purposes, lose their relationship with their children. Further, his present wife may berate him for not being firmer with his ex-wife. She may taunt him, saying that he turns into a wimp whenever the former spouse calls. Added to this are his thoughts and fears that the former spouse is making his child hate him. All of this combines to give the absent father a heavy dose of guilt.

A woman in a relationship with a divorced father also experiences guilt. Taking the time on weekends to try to build a relationship with his children and participate in other activities can make a woman feel guilty about the time she spends with her own children. The guilt is intensified for the career woman, who must have energy not only to work at her profession, but who is also expected to give time to her man, to her children, and, to his children.

The result is that a new brand of guilty female has emerged. She is bright, professionally successful, and personally tired. She considers herself a failure in the home because she has little time to have easy, loving, unstructured, caring, female time with her children. She feels that she never does enough at her job, for her children, or for her man.

Children feel guilt over the conflicting loyalties that they may feel toward both of their parents and their stepparents. They may like their stepparent, but suffer intense guilt that this liking is, somehow, traitorous to their parent. It goes like this: "If I love you (the stepparent) that means I don't love my mommy/daddy."

People don't feel guilty unless they *care*. It is my hope that this book will give you the tools to channel the energy wasted in guilt into a more constructive outlet.

10. Overindulging the children is a temptation to be resisted.

The complaint of many women in step is that their former spouses overindulge their children during visitation. The issue at stake is difficult for many women whose children live with them to understand. The custodial mother feels a closeness with her children that grows out of daily contact and from sharing the minor tasks of daily living. Thoughts of the children and of their habits come naturally, because they are consistently part of each other's lives. Because she is constantly present in her child's life, however, the custodial mother maybe unable to understand the fears of the absent parent.

The absent parent often feels that he has lost his place in his children's lives, and he feels the need to "play catch-up," regarding love, influence, values, education, and other matters. Should he discipline his children if he only sees them an average of five days a month? Is it fair to reprimand them? How can he handle their negative behavior? He fears, either consciously or unconsciously, that he may do something to drive his children even further from him. He is also concerned that their biological mother will brainwash the children and blow whatever he does out of proportion.

Women aren't immune to the dangers of overindulging their children. The last few years have seen greater numbers of women giving up custody or sharing custody with their ex-husbands. These women suffer from the same fears and compensating behavior that men have long experienced.

Shared custody doesn't offer a solution to the problem, for parents are placed in an even more vulnerable position as their children alternate between homes. The opportunity to play both parents against each other may increase the tendency for both parents to overindulge the child.

The solution to the very real problem of overindulgence would appear to be simple: Don't overindulge your children. Enforcing that rule may be hard, however. We want to show our love as much as possible, and if we can't be with our children all the time, we have to show love as intensely as we can in the short time that we have. Indulgences are a swift way of meeting that goal—but ultimately destructive. Instead, relationships have to be developed and communication has to be opened up that will allow us to communicate our love without failing to parent. Chapters 11 and 12 are devoted to this subject.

11. Money is a weapon of war in step.

Our society has come to see money as being equal with love,

and we are often valued according to our financial worth. In the step relationship, money is *always* an issue.

The second wife often sees herself as financially second best. She wonders why her husband feels that he must give his children more money than the divorce agreement calls for. Deliberately or otherwise, she may remind him that they have not gone on vacations. She may resent having to work to keep them financially solvent. She often finds that her money is needed to keep the step relationship going financially because his money is being used to make alimony and child support payments. The second wife may feel that she not only must help pay for his kids, but she must also act as their maid when they visit.

In turn, the ex-wife and the children from the previous marriage may also feel that they are being cheated financially. The children come to feel that Mom doesn't have enough money, while Dad and his new wife are living it up. The new family in their father's life, the nuclear stepfamily, is seen as taking away money that the biological children view as being rightfully theirs. As children grow older, wills and insurance policies can become major weapons of war in step.

The man in the step relationship may feel overburdened. He sees himself as supporting not only his biological children, but his stepchildren, as well.

Money can make everyone in the step relationship feel wronged. Adults do not know the right financial moves to make in the step situation, and, because it is all too confusing and complex, they often fall into a pattern of avoidance or a lack of disclosure.

The step relationship comes with no financial guarantees for the future. Should the relationship break up, the law does not compensate stepparents for what may amount to years of service. It seems as though, no matter what you do regarding money in step, somebody will be hurt. One way to avoid this is for stepcouples to discuss carefully their financial obligations and allocations before marriage. Not only are prenuptial agreements in order, but a marriage contract that concerns disbursements of time, energy, and money should also be planned.

You will find that Chapters 15 and 17 are especially helpful in guiding you in identifying your financial obligations and in gaining help in enforcing the obligations of others in the step relationship.

12. Many people view stepparenting as a difficult situation that is to be avoided.

Parenting under ideal circumstances is a difficult enough task without the added complexities of the step relationship. Growing numbers of males and females are shying away from commitment to marriage and family, and even more shy away from the step relationship. The causes are numerous. The high divorce rate has meant that many people, at some time, have been involved in a dating step relationship. Those who have become involved in step and who have failed have found their energies and emotions drained and their careers taxed.

Another reason for the lessened appeal of stepparenting is the greater involvement of women in the workplace, which has been accompanied by a reduced desire to parent. Many women naturally have reservations about the effect that parenting, even stepparenting, will have on their careers, their relationships, and the quality of their lives.

There are also many women who have never parented and who become involved in relationships with men who have children. Many of these women have unpleasant step experiences that may lead them to decide to never have a baby. A good number simply refuse to marry in step.

Further, the high rate of divorce has made everyone cautious. Responsible and loving men and women worry that there will be even greater hurt all around if a step relationship should fail than in one in which no children are involved. They may be wrenched from children whom they have grown to love and who love them in return. As a result, there appear to be more people today who are abstaining from serious involvements, preferring to have only casual relationships or no relationships at all.

The saddest reason that many people do not become stepparents is the fear of being hurt if the relationship ends. The ex-stepmother or ex-stepfather often leaves the relationship with no legal rights where the child is concerned. Very often the stepparent simply is dissolved out of their stepchildren's lives after years of involvement and caring.

Such fears are not groundless. At an even higher rate than first marriages, step marriages break up every day, and many people are hurt. Yet, many step marriages *do* survive, and they produce substantial love, happiness, and contentment for the family members. There are many ways in which you can work together to identify the challenge and find the solutions in the step relationship. You have to approach the step relationship with a desire to work with your spouse, children, and stepchildren to make the situation a success. An important part of your task lies in debugging your relationship (Chapter 6), setting up your household properly (Chapter 7), and getting organized (Chapter 8).

After considering the realities of step relationships, with the many fears and obligations that they promise, why would anyone even think of entering such a relationship? There are many reasons, and they all have to do with the wonderful feelings that come from having a warm, loving and supportive family surrounding us. But, it doesn't just evolve. Nor is there any magic word to turn a diverse group of people with different opinions on just about everything into a family.

For too many years, the focus has been only on the problems of step, and few solutions have been offered. The time for a change has come. You already know the problems of step. Now, let's move on and begin to work out the solutions.

Chapter 4

PRE-STEP PREPARATION

The step relationship does not begin with remarriage or living together. The stressful realities of step actually emerge as soon as we start to rebuild our social lives—and return to that strange and awkward ritual: dating.

The pre-step period is important not only because it provides the transition from divorce or death to dating, but also because it is an opportunity to deal with your anger, depression, dependence, and other problems. It is in this period that children must be helped to deal openly with their feelings of loss. They are likely to be suffering from an array of feelings as bewildering as yours. They need you to help them work them out. It is also in this period that the details of visitation and other leftover business from the previous marriage should be established. Only after these have been dealt with can most of us enter freely into new relationships with a feeling of wholeness.

At times, the problems that crop up after divorce or death seem insurmountable. You'll be tempted to push them aside and just blunder on with life. But try to resist this temptation. If you wait to confront the difficulties, you just may find them cropping up at the most inopportune moments—for instance, when you are happily involved in what appears to be a successful new relationship. Can any of us take that risk?

For that reason alone, it is well worth your time to examine those needs that are specific to the period between divorce and dating, and to choose your solutions before entering into a step relationship.

Searching for the New Self

After divorce both parents need a support system of adults. Divorce makes some people want to stay *isolated.* You may start living only through the children. Unconsciously, you may try to make them your support system. Other divorced people go through what might be called a readolescence. This stage consists of an almost hyperactive social life. The divorced man or woman begins a frantic search for a new partner or partners.

After the breakup of a marriage, we feel lost and bewildered. Who are we without our mate, our marriage? Are we still desirable to the opposite sex? As we did in our formative teenage years, we go through a sometimes heartbreaking search for our own identities. We seek ourselves in the world and within our selves. *This phase is necessary and normal.* We need this time to mourn our loss.

It's important to note that after divorce, each partner's and the children's self-esteem may diminish. As adults, it is important to check ourselves to see that we are doing what we need to do to enhance our self-esteem. But not at the cost of our children. We must find the balance between taking care of ourselves too much and being martyrs to the children.

Anger

Whether we've handled our anger at the ex-spouse is one of the most important issues before step and after divorce. It is important to know that anger has a value. It creates the distance needed to separate. On the negative side, anger allows either former spouse to feel victimized. We expect the world to feel sorry for us. Instead of getting on with life, we stay stuck as the victim. We all know individuals who have been remarried or divorced for years and still have not effectively dealt with their anger toward the ex-spouse.

It's almost impossible to remain angry and still have hope. It is hope and faith in the world and life that enables the mother and father of a child actively and positively to nurture that child. At the Stepfamily Foundation I have seen countless adults still involved in hot and cold wars with their former spouses. Often these battles are acted out through the children. The children become messengers of old angers. Anger between prior spouses is, to say the least, understandable. It is sadly even fashionable. But . . . bad-mouthing of and angry behavior toward the child's other parent is almost always damaging to the child's emotional health. As responsible parents we must begin to deal with that anger. Acts of anger generally provoke retaliation, and that only pours fresh fuel on old fires.

Post-Divorce-Depression

Depression has been defined as anger turned inward. It is the feeling of being backed up against the wall, a loss of control. Most decisions involve action and thinking. After divorce, we often feel helpless and hopeless and immobilized. Sometimes we cannot act. Sometimes there is nothing we can do with the wife who delays visitation or the husband who shows up two hours late. All that is left for us is the decision of how we are going to *define* the situation. We can create depression by defining ourselves as not being in control.

What is being said here? Stiff upper lip? Fake it when you feel bad? We have a right to our emotions, don't we?

No! Not always. Not as a parent. It's okay—perfectly normal—to feel depressed. Do your darnedest to keep your feelings from infecting your children.

Mourning

It is important to note differences between divorce and the death of a spouse. In divorce the prior spouse remains, and we constantly confront the reality of that person. In death, we confront a different kind of loss, and also often the deified persona of the departed. Studies have shown that it is essential and beneficial to mourn in order to go forward. The widowed must go through the mourning process in order to come to grips with the anguish that comes with the death of a family or the death of a spouse.

The rituals of the Catholic wake and the Jewish custom of sitting shivah help to perform the valuable functions and benefits that deep mourning brings. Mourning is an equally important phase for a person newly divorced. Recent studies highlight the value of the healthy process of mourning. Successful mourning removes one from the mainstream of life to ponder one's place in the world and one's relationship with the lost person, allowing one finally to return to that mainstream of life having adjusted to the loss.

When your spouse has died mourning consists of a sometimes overwhelming process, during which the bereaved is preoccupied with the dead person. As healthy mourning proceeds, the obsession passes, leaving behind it an acceptance of life—and death—and the ability to go on with life.

When mourning goes awry, the rest of one's life suffers. Over a protracted period of time, the mourner can be so overwhelmed and obsessed that grief becomes debilitating and distorts much of the rest of his life. This, we find, happens more often in divorce than in death, since our society is more practiced in handling death than divorce, despite today's escalating divorce rate.

Recent studies have found that self-hatred is common in normal grieving, as are feelings of hibernationlike inertia, apathy, and numbness. While these feelings had previously been seen as indicators of mourning gone awry, that view has been refined, and these feelings are seen as a problem only when they are too intense or prolonged.

"Death does not end a relationship in the person's mind. Mourning requires that a person review a relationship, mull it over in memories, dreams, fantasies. This review is self-propelled; it happens spontaneously. This review performs an essential task, one at the nub of mourning," according to Mardi J. Horowitz, a psychiatrist at the University of California Medical School in San Francisco. "The review allows an update of a person's mental map of himself and his world, to adjust it to the reality of the loss," he says. "You scan your memory banks to see what is still relevant to your life; what is not. You want to know, 'What do I have to let go of? What will I have to find in someone else? What can I contain within me?' "

Grief in Children

According to a recent report from the National Report of Science Academy, a pattern of destructive grief can be exaggerated among children. For many young children losses are so painful and frightening that they are able to endure the strong emotions for only brief periods, alternately avoiding them so as not to be overwhelmed.

Children are also apt to express grief in disguised forms, such as aggressiveness or hostility, or misbehavior at school. Among children who are bereaved, this process of disguised grieving may continue for many years after the loss.

While there is no universal timetable for grieving in adults, the cycle normally runs its course in a year or two.

Taking Responsibility

Often one partner in the past or current relationship is more dedicated than the other partner. One partner believes he or she has given their all. When one gives and the other takes, the dependency still remains mutual. The person who does all the giving allows him/herself the distance of resentment. He/she does not have to take responsibility for what's really going on.

It's important to know what part we play in the break-up. We can then be forgiving and allow the children to forgive. So many of us who enter step relationships have not clearly dealt with the past. Many of us have little or no idea of the specific reasons why "things" didn't work out . . . other than that it was the other guy's fault. A powerful position from which to really be in charge of our lives is to assume, and yes, actually *take* responsibility for what happens to us. And then move on with the lessons we have learned.

Getting Prepared

There are many areas in which we need to develop strategies and strengths before entering a step relationship. Success in any of them does not come easily, but the benefits to future relationships make the effort worthwhile.

Organizing the Family

Organizational patterns within some single-parent families range from rigid to chaotic. Although no one pattern can be said to be typical, chaotic organization is more often the norm. This is hazardous to the family's well-being. Families that operate chaotically often reflect such chaos in their interpersonal dealings. Children need a sense of direction. Children need to know what is expected of them so that they can achieve a sense of security.

Such chaos is neither inevitable nor is it irreversible. You can eliminate chaos by letting your children know exactly what is expected of them. You can provide them the refuge of the familiar activities which create predictability and stability.

For example, children should be given routine tasks that place boundaries on their daily lives. The toys must go in the toybox. Children of a certain age must set the table. Others must clear the table. In short, they must be given guidelines to live by and be assigned predictable jobs. In this way their chaos becomes ordered, and a sense of certainty can begin to enter their lives. You can also apply some of the aids suggested in Chapter 8 for getting organized.

Helping Children to Develop People Resources

It is important that parents give their children permission to talk with other people about the death of a parent or about the divorce. Many children may be afraid to discuss these matters for a variety of reasons. In some cases, they may feel that talking about them may appear to be disloyal. And, if they appear to be disloyal, they may drive you away from them. They don't want to say the "wrong" things, so they often say nothing.

That isn't healthy for children. Your children must feel free to discuss their feelings with a variety of caring people in their lives.

We must actively and verbally give them permission to—and even see to it that they can—talk to grandparents and other people resources about their points of view on problems within the household. Children should not be expected to suffer silently with their problems, nor should they remain isolated. When you isolate your children, you diminish their ability to cope. Take a look at Chapter 16 for a more in-depth discussion of this topic.

One-Minute Praisings

It is not only the major changes that create pain but the daily routine of living that makes life difficult. Although your child's behavior may seem to be driving you to distraction, you can do something about it. Try using quick, short bursts of praise—one-minute praisings—the next time that your child exhibits behavior that you would like to modify. Praise desirable behavior rather than harping upon what has not been done. Too often, it is only a child's negative behavior that receives notice from us, while the unnoticed but highly desired positive behavior remains unmentioned. With the small amounts of time that most parents have available for disciplining their children, noticing the child's positive actions and praising them, even briefly, can be effective.

Also remember to separate the behavior from the child. It is possible to love the child while being unhappy about what he does. Make sure that he knows this.

Somewhere along the line after the divorce or death, before you begin to date, you and your child must admit and accept that neither of you is perfect. Children have to learn to forgive their parents for not being perfect parents and for not being able to keep the family together.

Parents must take the lead to guide and discipline. Parents must also realize that the loss of the intact biological family, whether through death or divorce, is traumatic for children. They were never perfect before (although we might not have noticed it as much), and being thrown into the one-parent situation doesn't help matters any. Children cannot be perfect any more than their parents can. Everyone involved has to adjust to the new dynamics of their life, sort through their new roles and obligations, and begin to construct new lives that will make them more satisfied and fulfilled human beings.

This process is important to the success of all future relationships, and especially the step relationship. Entering the step relationship is difficult enough when one has strong self-esteem and feels secure in his/her identity. When the parent and child have not achieved this self-knowledge and have failed to determine their roles within the confines of the changed biological family, step can be a painful experience.

Preparing before the process begins is vital.

Chapter 5

DATING . . . THE FIRST STEP IN "STEP"

Dating Today

There are probably more people involved in dating situations today than in any other time in history. The social scene is blooming with a variety of eligibles from almost every generation. Joining the standard dating crowd is a mixed bag of seasoned adults and single parents, ranging in age from their thirties to their sixties.

The current dating scene reflects a merging of trends from the past twenty years. As a result, the parties bring into these relationships contradictory life styles and value systems. This is evidenced in dating situations where single parents and single nonparents (many of the women as young as their late twenties) continue to run into conflict as they endeavor to balance careers, children, and expectations of a new family.

As a result of the high divorce rate, delayed marriage, and the woman's movement, the high number of women in the work force, dating today has often become *a matter of step*.

So complicated is the dating scenario that trying to arrange a date is like putting together a jigsaw puzzle—there are so many elements to the whole picture. One of the most important and confounding elements is the children . . . where do they fit in and how? This single question changes the dating game into a contest of romance versus reality.

Romance Versus Reality

When you begin to date you initiate the dynamics of the step relationship. Whatever you believe, however you may try to keep them out of it, your children will influence your dating relationship.

Just the mention that you have children may separate the winners from the losers among potential dates. While the majority of people would claim to love other people's children at a distance, they are not always eager to test this feeling up close. The responsibility and the often unpleasant stories that circulate about the step relationship make many people run.

And it is not only men who run at the mention of children in a woman's life. Men with children often fare no better when they mention their children to the women they are dating. Although the situation for men is often easier because the majority of children still live with their mothers, the time to meet *his* children is often the time for *her* to take a walk.

Fortunately, though, not everyone vanishes at the mention of children. Some people welcome a "ready-made" family. For others, the prospect is simply something that will have to be dealt with at the appropriate time. For this latter group, what constitutes the "appropriate time" varies. Often it is best to delay meeting the children until a serious commitment is established.

The Commitment Avoiders

Commitment avoiders fall into two categories: those who don't date and those who do. Dating as a single parent presents a risk that dating as a single individual never did. In addition to the many other things that may go wrong with a relationship, there are also the dynamics of the children to consider. The success or failure of a marriage may rest on the extent to which the complexities associated with children are ironed out. Many single parents are afraid to risk another failure.

The result is that many single parents allow guilt over their children to intrude on their social life. When they dare to date, they often exhibit an approach/avoidance behavior, and their emotions range from hysteria to inertia. They alternate between feelings of "I don't care" and "I don't dare."

There are other single parents who date frequently and with fervor. Yet, they don't and won't even consider a serious relationship. Those of the "let's change partners and dance" school date as though children pose no problem. They have been there before, have been burned, and they don't want to reinvest in the charred territory of the past.

Although men are traditionally more notorious for being commitment avoiders, greater numbers of women have joined their ranks in recent years. Not only are women now establishing themselves professionally, with little need for the dubious security that a marriage—any marriage—offered in the past, but women have become increasingly aware of the complexities and demands of step dating and step marriage.

The overt commitment avoider is easy. Sam and Sandra are two typical examples of "no commitments, please."

Sam

He is tall, handsome, funny. He loves women. He is a talented cinematographer. Sure, he ignored his wife. Perhaps too often. She left him. He still mourns his loss. "She took my kid and moved with my beautiful daughter a thousand miles away. She took my house and now I have to live in a small apartment. Life has never been the same since she left with everything. My beautiful, beautiful daughter is too busy to see me. And I pay the money for child support and have no money for fun. My only child, my family . . . the divorce, the miles, and the money are killing me. I'll *never* commit to a marriage again . . . *never.*"

Sandra

Her beauty, energy, and wit stop traffic. Her voice enraptures. She gets results, and one thing is for sure: She's very smart. She was remarried for ten years to a famous American family . . . for ten years she dutifully stepmothered the two boys. All the resentments, all the hurts, all the efforting, all the good times ended. Ten years and a divorce. They never called her; she never calls them. With all his money she was compensated less than the maid for her years of caring. Now when she dates men with children she won't become involved with them. As soon as the man gets too close with his children she exits. She'll never *step* again.

In the secret world of the step wounded exist millions of people like Sam and Sandra. Many are not consciously aware of their fear to recommit. In this population of the divorced, redivorced and step, the scars of hurt run deep.

The covert commitment avoiders are trickier to identify. The story of Don provides some insight.

"Me or Them?"

Don described himself as a casual commitment avoider. When he found someone, his relationship lasted for a good period of time, sometimes for years. At fifty, he was glamorous, successful. One of the best catches in town. He had been dating for years. His two children visited and one was in college. Women his age with children always seemed to fall for him too quickly. He was suspicious. It was his money. They were too domestic, too old, too unattractive. He adored women in their late twenties, early thirties who had never been married.

It always ended up the same way. He fell in love, and she said, "You spend too much time with your kids—me, or them."

He always chose the kids. Don is still looking.

The Commitment Shoppers

Commitment shoppers want so much to find that committed partner that they often try too hard. Too soon in a relationship, they begin to plunge their new partner into the parent role. They involve the children and share all of their problems early in the relationship. The new partner becomes a confidante, substitute spouse and substitute parent—all when the dating relationship has barely begun. Rushing like this often produces the opposite result for the parent who seeks commitment. It is a classic step dating problem.

Too Much Too Soon: Sally

The date with John was no exception. The two had gone to dinner several times, but John had only picked Sally up at her apartment on the evenings that her son was out with his grandmother. On the evening of a lovely dinner party to which he was taking her, Sally invited John over to her place early, with the offer of cocktails and talk. He arrived on time and found Sally's son at the door to greet him while Sally called out from the bedroom that she was almost ready. While he waited, she suggested that he let her son entertain him.

Surveying what appeared to be wreckage of a hurricane around him in the living room, which was covered with toys, John was amply entertained. More than that, he was shocked. He could barely step across the room without stepping on a toy, or part of a toy. All the while, his guide talked incessantly beside him.

A few minutes after his arrival, Sally emerged from the bedroom, looking radiant but frazzled. Apologizing for the delay, she promised that she would only be another minute and told John to make himself a drink while her son switched on his favorite television show.

We often find that parents become myopic in their view of family life and of their own families. They dream about a romantic model based on their personal expectations and have difficulty realizing that not everyone outside their family will find that model acceptable. Many single parents merely expect other people to welcome their attempts to include them in the normal rhythms and activities of the family. They may be hurt when their kind offers to join in are refused. While the desire to develop closeness between a partner and one's children may be sincere, forcing an outsider to plunge into family life is not only unfair—it may be just plain bad manners.

"Some People Hate Children": Jim

Jim, a noncustodial father of two children, aged eight and ten, had spent every Friday night and several evenings a week for the past three months with Jennie, a never-married nonparent. As a man who was comfortable with his children, he had no doubt that others were also comfortable with them. For this reason, when his former wife asked if they could spend the night with him while she took care of her ill father, he didn't hesitate to have them stay with him.

The night happened to be one that he was to have dinner with Jennie. Rather than cancel, Jim felt that this would be a nice, spontaneous way for the three most important people in his life to meet. He called Jennie at her office to confirm the time of dinner and the restaurant at which they would meet. Almost too casually, he added, "Honey, I know that you won't mind that I have to bring my kids along tonight." How could she mind? So she agreed.

At dinner, the children refused to touch their food and clamored for his attention. Their unruly behavior brought numerous disapproving looks from other diners, although Jim seemed oblivious to the fact.

Later that evening, when they spoke on the phone after Jim had dropped Jennie off and the children were asleep, he asked her how she had enjoyed the evening. Since they had been straightforward with each other up to that point, Jennie leveled with him. She told Jim that the behavior of the children had left a bad taste in her mouth and that the evening had been no fun. She pointed out that they had been unruly and that they had monopolized all of his attention.

Jim became defensive and told Jennie that she didn't seem to like children. "If anyone acted like a child, it was you. It's your problem, and you'd better solve it!"

These examples may be upsetting, but they happen very often in the dating lives of single parents. So eager are many to reestablish the feeling of family that they subject their partners to overkill.

How Do You Date?

Is step dating only a matter of trial and error—or are there some guidelines to follow? If you want some help in your present situation, don't think back to high school, college or your early years of singlehood for models. They won't work. Now that you are a single parent, either previously married or not, male or female, the parent of one child or more, none of the old rules apply.

First of all, you will now be dating people from a greater age range than before. In the past, your educational environment may have determined the types of people you met and married. They were in your classes, involved in social events linked with your school, or struggling as new professionals, as you were. Having been out in the world for a while, professionally and personally, your range of contacts has broadened and so has your range of prospects. No longer are you limited to just one age group or profession.

That's the good news. The bad news is that being a parent, as well as a desirable and sexually experienced man or woman, you don't have the luxury of making your loved one your everything. Reality has to intrude and the stars have to leave your eyes.

At the casual dating level, most couples will do what all couples who are dating do. They will feel attracted to each other. They will enjoy each other's company. They may even fall madly in love with each other. As most of us do when blinded by romance, even single parents and their partners will tend to overlook the potential problems and obstacles. Instead, because even finding someone who genuinely cares for you and for whom you genuinely care is so difficult, the feeling is often that love will triumph over even the biggest problem and make all the bad go away.

It doesn't, of course. And, at the casual dating level, we don't have to worry too much about it.

Such warm expectations are cooled soon enough as certain problems begin to emerge when one partner is a parent. It is never really just the two of you—the reality of the child or children is always there, intruding on the privacy of the relationship, however subtly. Although the parent may choose to keep his children out of the dating relationship, children manage to involve themselves both emotionally and physically in a variety of ways.

Dating as a single parent initiates a wide range of problems, or "trouble spots," which differ substantially from dating in the previous, pre-parenting life. Time management, sex, the presence of a frequently unwanted new person in the established family unit, the new image of Mommy or Daddy as an adult with a life of her/his own, and the role of the children in the dating relationship present some difficult questions that don't always have satisfactory answers.

Dating the Woman Who Is a Single Parent

The man who dates a woman who has children faces several major problems. He may be unfamiliar with the care and handling of children. One reason may be that he may have never married, or married and not had any children. In some cases, a man who is a noncustodial parent may rarely see his children. As a result, he is not aware of how children behave on a day-to-day basis nor is he familiar with the range of their emotional reactions to even minor incidents. Because he loves their mother, he may want desperately to be for them the male figure whom he sees that their lives lack.

He will generously provide them with guidance, assistance, and instructions—only to see them turn their backs on him. Their mother may want him to help her with the children because she may feel guilty about her lack of time for mothering. She may let him know, either through words or actions, that she needs him to give them time and love. Yet the children may constantly reject his efforts. For the man who seriously dates and loves a woman with children, a bedeviling "Catch 22" situation evolves.

When the woman has a son with whom she is very close, the situation becomes volatile. The man may find that he will be looked upon as a rival for the mother's affection, an outsider between his lover and the son who has fancied himself to be the mother's protector and companion—"the man of the house." While the man may recognize the special bond that the mother and son share, he will also begin to resent playing what may amount to only a secondary role. From somewhere deep and unknown within him, there will arise anger that will make him lash out at his lover or her son for minor incidents. His lover may lavish mother love and adoration on her son, unwittingly placing her man in the role of second best.

Grownups, as well as children, can and will behave irrationally. Such behavior may come as a surprise to those around them. A man will find it difficult to admit that he is jealous of the attention that the woman he dates gives to her children. To admit that would appear to be immature, and he doesn't want to be seen in that light. Even when he clearly plays second fiddle to the woman's children, a man will often suppress his anger and just let it continue until the pressure becomes too much. Then, rather than admitting to the problem, he will more than likely just fade out of the picture and say that "things didn't work out," or lash out and disappear.

There is an alternative, but it isn't easy. The man who dates a woman with children must take a hard look at the relationship if it is floundering and identify the trouble spots. He must begin to learn the rules, the behavior, and the dynamics of the new romantic game of step to help him in identifying the pitfalls. Most of all, he has to communicate his annoyance, his anger, and his fears to the woman he loves. If the relationship is important to them both, they can begin solving the problems.

Dating the Man Who Is a Single Parent

Changes in custody arrangements have meant that greater numbers of men are gaining custody of their children than ever before. Even for those who don't, a greater move toward joint custody has emerged. In addition, many fathers with visitation privileges tend to involve the women they date in the visitation. The effect that such arrangements have on dating is substantial.

The most important confrontation often occurs during the first date in which the children are included. What starts out to be a pleasant experience often turns out to be a rude awakening, with both the children and their father's lover upset by inadequate attention from the father. The father will generally pay more attention to his children than he will to the woman in his life. He does this because of years of conditioning that tell him that his children must come first. Men have also been conditioned to feel that women like to see a man who is attentive to his child.

That is a false expectation in the dating relationship. Both his lover and his child want to come first in his life. Faced with guilt over the broken marriage, or the feeling that he is only a part-time parent, if the arrangement is either joint custody or visitation, the father may feel a need to supply his child with more attention than the child actually needs. He often plays "catch up" or spoils his children while his lover burns.

Even more troublesome in such relationships is the tendency of the less-than-full-time father to enjoy, educate, and indulge his child during the little time that they have together in the presence of his lover. He feels that the little time spent together should not be "wasted" in discipline. So, while his lover may endure in stony silence, the children have their way, behave badly, act ill-mannered and rude, and talk back to their father.

Such a situation would justifiably drive many women away, unless both partners in the step dating relationship honestly want to make it work. One of the major problems in this situation is that the etiquette of step dating has not really been established. Remember that women have traditionally been the social arbiters both in the home and in society. Until recently, women had the greater contact with children and decided how children were to behave. They gave love to the child at the designated times and set the limits at others. Women created the emotional environment of the family.

Once left to deal on their own with a child, men are often at a loss as to how to proceed. They have no models for how to be a divorced father. As a result, they may seek assistance outside of themselves with a woman and hope that their new woman will have the same understanding as a mother would. She often doesn't. She frequently isn't a mother—and she certainly isn't his child's mother. More likely, she comes to the situation with a romantic notion of their relationship, wanting him to be her Prince Charming.

This makes for a sticky situation. The single father has to realize that he cannot have the same expectation of the woman he dates as he might of the child's mother. Just because his date is a female and has the right biological equipment doesn't mean that she is going to mother or have the attributes of the mothering/nurturing person. There may be women who can slip into the role without much preparation, but expecting women in general to do so is unrealistic.

Establish a standard of behavior for the child. Rules, decorum, and manners to be maintained in the company of the new person should be clearly spelled out. Further, both the father and his lover have to discuss just how they will handle their dating relationship and where they hope it will lead.

What If You Have Never Parented?

The single nonparent who dates a man or woman with children may have the most romanticized view of family life of all. Because they have not had firsthand experience with some of the more trying aspects of marriage, parenting, and stepparenting, most may hold numerous romantic notions. Worse, they may not know how inaccurate many of their perceptions can be.

Once a single nonparent begins to date a man or woman with children, all of the old notions lose their credibility. The situation is more complex than one of dating just another person, and loving one man or woman is not enough. Suddenly, there are children who are also clamoring for your lover's attention and, by extension, for yours. Dating a single parent may become more than you bargained for—or more than you want to deal with.

At best, dating a single parent becomes a juggling act of mixed emotions and contrary actions. You are asked to understand a lot of behavior; you are charged with the responsibility of making allowances for everyone's past and present problems.

If the relationship is not important to you, the best advice anyone can give you is just to leave it before the children, your lover, or you become too attached. If you want to make the relationship work, then you will have to look at it and assess carefully your complaints about the step dating situation. Communicate your feelings to your lover, the single parent. You will have to learn new information and develop strategies that will help the relationship to survive.

Making Dating Successful

The main ingredient of any step dating relationship is the child or children of one or both partners in the relationship. Without them, of course, there is no step relationship.

The First Date with the Children: Friends

Remember, children are less threatened by friends. A parent's new "friend" is a lot easier for a child to accept than a parent's new lover. Children are experts at picking up your "charge" and special attitude about this person—so try to act more like a friend than a lover when the children are with you.

Plan a short period of time for the first date with the child along. Some ice cream, pizza, or a sandwich in a comfortable place. Something like "my new friend Jane; I met her at my —— class. She'll meet us at the zoo, and we'll have some ice cream with her after."

Generally, it's good to keep the first encounters short, even if they are going well. We advise that parents integrate and socialize their children with a number of adult friends, whether they are sexual partners or not. This way the child will feel comfortable with adults, and this will diffuse the sexuality of any given situation. After divorce or death the child's relationship with the parent may become fragile. Seeing the noncustodial parent can reawaken the scary feelings surrounding the divorce.

Often, when the child sees the parent (custodial or noncustodial) with a potential new partner, the emotions connected to loss are reawakened and the child fears another loss. In order to save the remaining parent, the child may try to alienate the new threatening foreign power. Again, as much as we may think that the child is conscious of his behavior, he is not. Ask the child about his behavior and the answer will vary from no answer at all to something completely off the mark.

First Date with the Child: More than Friends

The child knows or suspects that there is something more to this relationship than just friendship. Once again, the first meeting is important. Both your lover and your child may demand your attention. Beware of thinking that the two of them will figure this out. You cannot give both of them your undivided attention. *You* must sort it out. The biological parent is responsible and is the key factor in making this first date comfortable and successful.

Beware of focusing too much on the child and expecting your lover to understand. Just like a formal, old-fashioned dinner party: It's fifteen minutes of conversation to the dinner partner on the left and then fifteen minutes of conversation to the right. Be careful about leaving people out . . . you'll pay for it later. Also inform your adult companion of the dynamics of outsiders and insiders and the conflicts of dealing with "who deserves most of my attention." Decide who deserves your first answer when both ask you a question at the same time. Prioritize and inform. This goes back to simple etiquette. Children do not interrupt adults, and since adults are adults they command the privilege of being responded to first.

Activities. Here again the parent generally decides, but carefully discuss it with your partner. The activity could be something that will bring you all together and something everyone can enjoy. A movie is a good example. After the activity, it's a good idea for everyone to talk about it. Perhaps over a slice of pizza or an ice cream. Remember, go slow.

Dealing with Children's Questions and Feelings

Children frequently ask right from the beginning: "Are you going to marry him (her)?" Find out the child's opinion. Often a child desperately wants a parent to be happy and remarry. Some children interview every date for the role. Check and see if the child has picked up any negative notions about step.

The child may express his dislike in two different forms. He may openly dislike your friend because of his/her personality, or he may unconsciously show dislike because this potential partner is in the position of preventing the child's parents from getting back together. Be careful. Children often do not know that they are responding to the potentially threatening position this person holds rather than to his/her personality.

Get feedback. Talk about the stability of the child's life as a part of your life. The parent's job is the toughest. In the beginning, the parent carefully watches attitudes. The parent is the host, and it's the parent's responsibility to oversee the comfort of both the child and the potential partner. In addition, tell the child what to expect and what is expected from him. Your date and you might discuss expectations and plans for handling discipline. Remember, beginnings set precedents.

Discipline Problems

Children don't always behave. They test us. Generally, their job in life is to learn in school and to see how far they can push adults' boundaries. This is natural. In the case of many widowed and divorced parents, children succeed in pushing us too far for their and our own good. Children get away with bad behavior for a multitude of reasons: the parent's guilt over divorce, lack of time and/or quality time, and lack of energy for discipline. Very often the child has already set a precedent of winning over the adult and overcoming the parent's boundaries. For parents, it all adds up to no good for nobody.

Prepare the children. Just as you would prepare the child for a bar mitzvah, or for the ceremony of being a flower girl at a wedding or for attending a formal affair, prepare the child for appropriate manners at the restaurant or outing. Show the child how to shake hands, how to look someone in the eye, when to stand up and sit down, and how to handle hellos and good-byes.

Today, many single and working parents feel they do not have the time to teach manners. Many don't even know them. Read Emily Post or Miss Manners.

Remember your date is not a member of the family. Discipline is low-voiced, authoritative and gentle. Dating and discipline simply require us to be more elegant at getting the behavior we need from our children.

Sotto voce . . . with intention and preparation ahead of time. Should the child continue to act out, quietly mention the consequences, and carry them out later. A parent needs to get accustomed to getting polite behavior from a child. Structure and guidance equal love and nurturing.

Often parents are accused of "not seeing" the bad manners and sulky behavior of their children. How does a date handle the parent when he/she feels the child has been impolite or even rude?

Answer: in the beginning, as gently and as little as possible. When you and your single-parent date are alone, you might ask if he/she noticed that the child did this or that. If he/she saw nothing, heard nothing, and knew of nothing, step back. Find out the emotional temperature of the parent. Is he or she playing catch up? Is the parent afraid of losing the child's favor? Is the parent afraid to discipline?

If the child's behavior should continue or even worsen and the parent believes it to be "your fault," you do have a problem. The date is a victim of circumstance, and this is a classic step problem. The challenge now is good communication with the parent— without making the parent or the child wrong. Encourage the parent to notice behavior. Once this behavior can be recognized, the two of you can set forth to delineate expected behavior. This is a true step challenge and often better done with the help of a trained counselor.

In addition to discipline and the avoidance of classic step scenarios, such issues as money, sex, vacations, and the eventualities of further contacts and commitments must be worked out. Each issue has an appropriate time and place for discussion and decision. Some decisions you will make as parents, and others you'll make together with your lover.

The major issue in step dating, after the couples' own development, is the relationship with the children. You'll have to work hard to avoid the negative dynamics of step by knowing them and doing something about them . . . at the appropriate time.

What You See May Be Only Half of What You Get

Once you feel that you want to make a commitment—with this person and at this time—then you should begin to examine how you can make that commitment successful.

Romantic evenings spent holding hands, dining out, dancing and making love are good for the body and the soul. Nonetheless, they don't always provide people with a realistic view of each other's perceptions of family life and their approach to the raising of children—the stuff of which lasting and sound step relationships are made.

The romance of dating is fun, and physical, intellectual and emotional attraction between the two adults is vital in a step relationship. Beyond this, however, there exist a variety of realities in step that intrude rather quickly upon the romantic vision when people establish a serious relationship.

If you are the biological parent, you must suddenly go from a life in which you were the controlling adult who set the pace in the family to a life in which you must compromise with another adult and parent and agree in setting new rules. As the nonparent in the relationship, you may be experiencing family life, and stepfamily life for the first time as an adult. This, indeed, may be double trouble unless you educate yourselves. You will have to begin assuming two new roles, those of spouse and stepparent. Even if you are a noncustodial parent, you will be forced to change your life drastically as you have to compromise with another adult and deal with the needs of a stepchild.

We've all grown up in families that have their own rules, roles, and regulations. Because of this, we each come to marriage with a different view of what constitutes family life. What the mother does in one family may be the function of the father in another. Children may be constantly seen *and* heard in one family, but required to exhibit great restraint around grownups in another.

These differences in what each partner expects in the step-family can be a cause of pain and hostility for all members of the family. Feelings are hurt and chaos results without clearly defined expectations. The problems that Rachel encountered are typical in this respect.

"Who's In Charge Here?"

John and Rachel had the best of intentions. They were only married six months when John finally won a yearlong custody battle with his ex-wife, who now lived in California. The children had lived a chaotic life. Their mother had been running around with an assortment of men, pulled the children out of several schools, taken only odd jobs, and generally done her own thing.

On the day that they won custody, John rejoiced, Rachel cried. As soon as the school year was over, John flew out and picked up the children. The children arrived in New York angry, and John came back looking tired.

Nothing went right from the first day that thirteen-year-old Jill and ten-year-old John arrived. The older child adored her father but had no hesitation in telling Rachel that she didn't have to obey anyone who was not her mother.

John and Rachel began to fight. He said that she was too tough on the children and that the problem was hers and she had better learn to deal with it. Rachel told him that he never backed her up. In fact, he seemed to side with the children more than with her.

After working so hard to obtain custody, John began to feel that he was losing his family for a second time. To avoid confrontations, he began to stay later at the office. Rachel increased her complaining. She began to resent not only the children but also John's absences and lack of support and affection. On Saturdays, he expected her to spend time with the children while he worked.

The situation worsened until the two had a major fight and both threatened to leave. It was then that they decided to seek our help.

Central to the difficulties that Rachel and John experienced was their failure to assess their individual expectations *before* they became a stepfamily. Neither of them understood their own perceptions of what each family member was supposed to do. As a result, neither could help the other in assuming their fathering and stepmothering roles within the context of their other work and responsibilities.

It is natural that role expectations may differ, and that the experiences you and your partner have will give you a different view of the way a family runs. You can't fall into step the way you fall into love without receiving some serious bruises. The way in which you spend your time, your expenditure of energy, and your allocations of money must change when you seriously commit yourself to a step arrangement.

You will take on a new role, going from single mother to mother and wife, or to mother, wife, and stepmother. Your role as single father will become father and husband, or father, husband, and stepfather. You may go from being a nonparent whose life is guided by a flexible schedule to being a spouse and stepparent or spouse, stepparent, and natural parent.

You and your partner may not view all of these roles in the same way. Nor will you agree as to the way in which time, energy, and money are to be managed in the stepfamily. These are important issues, which must be examined and worked out. No couple thinks alike in all areas. You do, however, have to be willing to listen to and to begin to understand the way that the other person thinks. Only then will you be on the road to a successful stepfamily relationship.

It is easier to operate when you have some already established rules and regulations to which you can refer. Working out those rules and regulations, although it can be done after you are already experiencing the problems, is easier when done before you begin tripping all over each other.

While you are planning your new arrangement, you will be more objective, less emotional; and more open to negotiation than you will be if you are trying to set guidelines while sitting in the middle of a sticky situation.

One of the greatest problems of step relationships is that of unclear job descriptions and expectations. It is also one that can be eliminated at the outset. Setting guidelines early is beneficial to everyone.

You may have to compromise, but such compromise is for the good of the step relationship. And that should be everyone's goal.

Chapter 6

DEBUGGING THE RELATIONSHIP

You bring into a relationship a view of the family that is drawn from a number of vantage points. Your expectations of the roles of men and women, the roles of adults and children, the roles of wives and husbands may vary greatly from another individual's expectations. Cultural and ethnic differences color these perspectives. The diverse experiences of your life will further distinguish your view of roles and the family from those of other people.

Your Notion of the Family

Before combining with another person to create a new family, it's a good idea to think about what your expectations for the family are. What were your notions of family life as you were growing up? What was your notion of the family when you were first married?

Finally, what is your notion of the stepfamily? The following exercise can help you to understand the similarities and differences between you and your partner.

Exercise—Notion of the Family

Instructions

The couple should respond to this exercise separately; then compare responses after the exercise is completed. Feel free to write down ideas as they come to you in random order. Take seven minutes. Write as fast as you can. Let your ideas flow. All answers are correct. Enjoy your recollections.

I. What was your notion of the family while you were growing up? What did children do? What did grownups do? What did fathers do? What did mothers do? Who made the decisions? What were the major decisions? How were chores handled? How were the issues of money, anger, family upsets, rituals, religion, etiquette, and meals handled?

_____

_____

_____

_____

_____

II. If you were married before, what was your notion of the family in your first marriage? Respond to the issues listed in the first question.

_____

_____

_____

_____

_____

III. What is your perception of the stepfamily now?

_____

_____

_____

_____

_____

How would you want it to be?_____

_____

_____

_____

In a step relationship, whether married or living together, the couple really needs to find itself and to define what its expectations are for the relationship. Human relationships are complex, and they become even more complex when they involve stepchildren. This is very hard, because many of us look to our notion of traditional family as a model.

Pull of Blood versus Sexual Energy

In a step relationship, one of the involved adults is not a biological father or mother. Therefore, two different forms of energy exist in the relationship. These are the pull of the sexual energy and the pull of the blood energy, or the pull of the couple towards each other and the pull of the parent toward the child. These two are in conflict in a step relationship, while this is seldom the case in the intact biological family. It is important that two people who are seriously considering a commitment realize that these pulls and conflicts are also classic issues in step and that they prepare themselves to deal with them.

The Time, Energy, Money Grid

An important tool that can be used to clear up misconceptions *before* making a serious step commitment is the Time/Energy/ Money Grid. This tool helps both members of the couple to examine what they believe should be their contributions of time, energy, and money to the step relationships. In the same way, each can see what the partner views as his/her own role in these areas. When the two sets of expectations are compared, important areas that need work may be identified. These concerns are important to the step relationship and have to be clarified to avoid shocks to the relationship after commitment.

The first area of concern before deciding to live together or to marry is the *home* and evaluating what each partner sees as his basic contribution. What does a home consist of? What makes it work? Who will bring the couches, the rugs, the china, and other items? Where do the responsibilities fall for indoor and outdoor maintenance? What percentage of time should go into upgrading the home and whose responsibility is it? Where will the basic responsibilities lie for general running of the home, i.e., shopping, cooking, entertaining, cleaning, home maintenance and taking care of in-house or visiting children.

A more sensitive issue in regard to our expectations around the establishment of the home is that of money. In our culture, talking about money is difficult. Money is unromantic. Money is a bad thing. Nonetheless, money is important in step relationships, no matter how wealthy the participants may be. It is important to multimillionaires. It is important to those with limited incomes. It is important to people on all social and economic levels.

To a great extent, money in our culture has come to be equated with how much people care. Money signifies how much we love. In a step relationship, money also stands for energy and symbolizes how much of our energy, the product of our labor, we will put into the relationship. So, an important consideration for the couple is how they expect to contribute financially to running the home. How will their contributions be divided? How much money will each put into maintenance? How much money will each contribute to normal operating expenses? To upgrading the home? To entertaining? To the children? To schooling and camp?

The next concern is the *couple*. As a stepcouple, new techniques of relating will be required. You will need to spend time, energy, and money, gather new tools, and learn to communicate better. You will have to work on your relationship. To do this, you have to assess the percentage of time that you expect to spend on the couple relationship, the percentage of energy you expect to expend, and the percentage of money you expect to expend.

A third concern is the *overall family*. What percentage of the total time, energy and money goes into the overall family? That can include parents, sisters, brothers, children, everyone. What do you see as each participant's appropriate contribution?

Another important area to consider is that of *career*. It's hard to have a family and a career and a new relationship all at once. To make it work, you and your partner have to examine the anticipated effect of each career upon the family. You need to know how you parcel out time, energy, and money, and how you intend to manage that in your relationship. You have to assess the costs in time, energy, and money of your career.

Expectations related to *children* are a critical area of evaluation. How much time, energy, and money do each of you expect to put into the children? What percentage of time should be spent as caretaker? How much time, energy, and money do you expect to spend in guiding the children? Who should take his, her, and their children to cultural experiences? What percentage of your time, energy, and money will you put into learning experiences?

A major source of concern is the *prior spouse*. What percentage of time do you feel should be spent in talking about, dealing with, and worrying about your partner's and/or your prior spouse? What percentage of your energy should your relationship with the prior spouse take up? What percentage of money will the prior spouse and her/his custodial children take up and take away from your current relationship?

Evaluating your expectations in this area and seeing how they compare with your partner's is important to establishing a successful step relationship. Obtaining such information before a serious commitment is made can avert later hostilities that can do even greater harm to the stepfamily.

Playtime is also important to the step relationship, and you should assess your feelings in this area before making a commitment. How much time, energy, and money do you feel you should expend in playtime with your partner? How much time, energy, and money should be spent in playtime with children? Whose children take priority? How much time should be spent in personal playtime?

The final area that should be evaluated is that of *learning and growth*. You need to know more about how you view relationships. What percentage of time, energy, and money should be spent in learning and growth and the building of a partnership that works?

Fill out the Time/Energy/Money Grid that follows by yourself. It's best to Xerox the grid and enlarge it. Then copy a second grid and write what percentages are compiled by your partner. Then compare all of your results with those of your spouse. This is a point-of-view exercise, and the amounts which you enter are to be totally subjective. Percentages need not add up to 100. Responses to this exercise should be those that feel right to you. For example, if you feel that you contribute 80 percent of the time in which housework is done, then you should write that figure down.

Time/Energy/Money Grid

Instructions. If possible, Xerox and enlarge the grid. In each of the columns, fill in the percent of time, energy, and money that you expect to contribute in each of the following areas in a step relationship. Estimate what you believe to be your partner's contributions. Each of you will have two documents to compare. Do not argue over differences. Honor the other's point of view and work toward agreement. This exercise is merely an example of how differently we see how a system works.

	Time	*Energy*	*Money*
HOME			
Basic Contribution			
Maintenance			
Inside work			
Outside work			
Upgrading			
Entertaining			
Meals			
COUPLE TIME			
OVERALL FAMILY			
Parents			
Sisters			
Brothers			
Children			
CAREER			
CHILDREN			
Your children (overall)			
As caretaker			
As guide			
In play			
Partner's children (overall)			
As caretaker			

As guide			
In play			
Our children (overall)			
As caretaker			
As guide			
In play			
PRIOR SPOUSE			
Yours			
Your partner's			
PLAYTIME			
With partner			
Alone			
With your children			
With your partner's children			
With our children			
LEARNING AND GROWTH			
Personal			
Joint			

Your Job—Or Mine?

Step people often do not know what their roles and responsibilities are within the stepfamily. Problems arise over seemingly unimportant questions such as "Who does the dishes?" and "Who picks up the children?" These may seem to be unimportant issues, and in the intact biological family they may be, but they take on major significance in the stepfamily.

Because each of the members of the step relationship brings different expectations and ways of doing things to that relationship, you cannot expect that everyone will immediately fit neatly into a specific role. They won't. In one family, children may be expected to share in the care and maintenance of the home. In another, they are free of all household duties and the parents emphasize a devotion to study and self-improvement. In still another family, children over a certain age may take on *all* of the household duties.

What, then, can be done to reduce the friction that a lack of familiarity with family roles can stimulate? Talk to each other. The adults in the relationship have to set the guidelines for the relationship before the situation can get out of hand. Children need to know where they fit in, and so do the adults.

Sit down with paper and pen. List each member of the step relationship on a separate piece of paper. Below each name, describe what you feel should be the role and the responsibilities of that member. For children, specify the way in which these roles and responsibilities differ with age and in accordance with their living arrangement, *i.e.,* in-house or visiting. Use the Job Description List below as a guide.

Job Description List

For the adults

1. What will be the financial contribution of each to the relationship?

2. What are the moral obligations of each to the relationship?

3. What are the household maintenance responsibilities, both indoors and out of doors, of each?

4. What are the mealtime obligations of each?

5. What are the responsibilities of each in regard to the discipline and guidance of children living in the home?

6. What are the responsibilities of each in regard to the discipline and guidance of children who visit?

7. What are the financial obligations of each?

8. What are the specific personal needs of each, apart from the step relationship?

For the children

1. How old is the child and what may be considered behavior appropriate to that age?

2. What are the child's academic obligations?

3. What are the child's extracurricular obligations?

4. What tasks within the home is the child expected to undertake?

5. What manners are expected of each of the family members? Parent? Stepparent? Siblings? Stepsiblings?

6. Who is responsible for the discipline of that child?

7. How will rewards and punishment be meted out?

8. What will the child's personal space consist of?

9. How much will the child be expected to share with in-house stepsiblings? With visiting siblings?

10. What are the child's specific rights within the step relationship?

Now compare your list with that of your partner. What are your job descriptions for the members of the potential stepfamily? What are your partner's? Do your expectations agree with those of your partner? If they don't, then you should discuss your differences in perception and work to create a clear understanding of what the job description of each family member should be.

Each of you puts together a list from your own perspectives and then combine those perspectives. Discuss job descriptions for the children *with* the children. Get their points of view. Motivate them. Now you and your partner have specific expectations for the relationship.

Now the male and female heads of the household can agree

upon a list, calling it, for example: Duties and Responsibilities. Rules of the Smith and Jones Household. The tentative list gets typed. Then a family meeting is held and the rules get posted on the fridge.

A/B Reality: The Honoring of Differences and the Beginning of Creating Couple Strength

I learned high school History in three different countries. The history was very different in each country. At first I naively made note to my teachers that other countries had different versions of the same story. They ignored me. Then I wrote a paper describing these differences. I got a reprimand—"This was not the assignment!"—and a low grade. So I stopped this comparison business. I decided that history was a point of view and not just the facts, and that it varied country to country, teacher to teacher.

Actually, this rude awakening was not such a bad thing. My divorced parents were still angry at each other. Each constantly told me a different story about the other. My school experiences helped me to deal with the conflicts between my parents. I began to view them just as having experienced history from different points of view. I was relieved of the awful curse, when children often are asked to take sides, of believing one parent over the other.

One of the most important tools we use here at the Stepfamily Foundation is our A/B Reality Tool. I draw two boxes—one with a big A and the other with a big B. I explain that each of us is programmed differently: A likes pink flowers, B likes red flowers. A does not like to sunbathe, B loves the sun. B argues, "A, you look great with a tan. Come with me to the beach and let's enjoy the sun together." "No," says A. "You, B, are a dope to lie in the sun."

Each tries to pull the other into their A or B Reality. Each argues their point of view. Arguments sometimes go on for days, even years.

It works to respect the other's point of view. We must create a C reality in a partnership. To do this, we take some from A's reality and some from B's reality. Agreements to disagree are agreements, and go into a C column until all is worked out.

Do this by never using the word "You." Language like, "You don't know what you're talking about! This is the reality!" is not allowed. Remember, we are learning to understand and speak different languages—Malese and Femalese. As in a foreign country, showing courtesy in any communication exchange, is imperative!

Use the words, "I feel . . . I see . . . I hear . . ." We own and honor the reality as our own. We recognize that the other is not wrong, but simply different.

The Lake Placid Exercise: How We See, Hear, Feel and Sort our Realities by People, Places, and Things

The following story also exemplifies differences. Now we look further into how our partner sees, hears, and feels the world, and how they sort their realities in terms of people, places, and things.

My husband is the usual guinea pig for these training exercises I learn at professional training seminars. Once, after skiing the whole day at Lake Placid, I asked him if he would endure an experiment that would take place during the journey from the door of the hotel to a restaurant where we were dining that night.

"Yes," he ughed. With a little trepidation, like the girl with the tea party story related in Chapter 9, I filled him in on what was to take place.

"We will see, hear, feel, and sort regarding people, places, and things—everything that takes place during this brief period, without talking or sharing our realities. We'll do that only when we sit down."

"Blessings," he cried, happy that this was to be such an uncomplicated exercise. We followed through with the plan and, once seated in the restaurant, he said, "You start." I did.

My Reality:

We went out of the hotel door. It was freezing cold. Ice was on the steps down to the car. He held my arm to help me into the car. "How nice," I thought. "I was falling all over the mountain during the day and he did not offer to pick me up. Well, we are both tough skiers." I was dressed for dinner. I remember nothing of the drive except that the night was black. We pulled into the parking lot and I could hear the gravel under the car wheels. We walked up the steps to the restaurant. A blond, buxom lady led us to our table. I smelled the room, thinking the food would be only mediocre, and looked around at the people—pretty mediocre also.

His Reality:

Interestingly enough, his memory didn't include helping me into the car or the drive to the restaurant. But, after getting to the restaurant through the pitch black of the night (my reality), he did notice how many other BMWs were in the parking lot and that the license plates were from different states. How many from Canada? Massachusetts? New York? Vermont? New Jersey? He didn't notice the blond lady who took us to our table.

How different we are. I would never have looked at the men— they spend so much time thinking about how they measure up to other men. Who else had a BMW? How far did others have to drive to get there? While I had heard the parking lot, he saw what was in it. What was I always thinking about? Feelings and people.

Instructions. Drive, walk, or go to an occasion and designate 15–20 minutes to not talking, but just being in the same place together. Then sit down and compare. Have fun!

Walk a Mile in the Other's Shoes—High Heels or Cordovans

This exercise involves actually becoming your partner's shadow in movement and in spirit. The two of you go for a walk. The walk must be in an area where there are people, stores, or things with which to interact. When your partner stares at something, you stare at the same thing. No matter how long she looks at something or interacts with someone, stand by her and observe. Attempt to feel what is going on with her. What is important to her? Why does she like to do this? What is nice for her? What is difficult for you? What insights do you have about you and your partner?

This is really getting to know each other by observing. So, *no* laughter, unless she does, and *no* putdowns. The follower's job is to be silent and to "be with . . ." The walker's job is to *be* herself and to do as she would normally do. As the follower, in the corner of your mind, as you're observing and giving most of your attention to the other, think about what you like and would want to do or say under the same circumstances.

Walk the way he walks. Look at what he looks at, feel what he touches. Image how he talks to a salesperson in a store. Stay right with him, saying nothing. Be his shadow. Your job is to learn, know, be like, *be* him. You see, hear, feel as he does.

Don't forget to have fun! This is your partner and you can find out astonishing similarities and dissimilarities in the way each of you views the world. We may not exactly understand our differences, but we can respect them.

Instructions. This exercise takes about 20 minutes each time. It can be done when you both go for a walk, to the mall, to the seashore, or other places you plan together. Each partner takes a turn. Compare your insights after each is finished. Enjoy.

Fite Fair

This technique is used by stepfamily professionals, but it can also be done by couples at home. It is used when a couple continues to fight about one subject that they seem unable to resolve. What is called for is what we call a "fite fair."

Instructions. The fite fair must be held in a totally safe space— after the children have gone to bed, in the basement, in the attic—someplace where the couple will not be disturbed. They go into the space, taking two equally sized chairs, pulling these up close to each other, sitting knee to knee. Both place their hands on their thighs, where the hands will remain so they aren't used in gesturing. Each looks the other partner in the eye and tries to breathe in sync. This is so that the messages come from soul to soul, heart to heart, with no movements or gestures that may allow one person to distract or dominate the other.

The person who called the fite fair begins talking. He can scream, he can yell, he can cry. The other must simply look him in the eye, breathe with him, be with him—and not move from the fite fair position. The person who begins can talk, as long as he or she wishes, and then when finished says, "I am finished." The other then begins. This partner talks as long as she wants to, and when finished, says, "I am finished." The other partner talks once again until finished.

Back and forth this goes, perhaps for 30 minutes. The time between "I am finished" should get shorter so problems can be dealt with, one by one. The couple must endeavor not to string together so many issues that either partner becomes confused or overwhelmed. About 30 minutes into the fite fair, the couple must go for a solution.

They continue to go back and forth until a solution is reached, and *they may not get up until they agree upon a solution, even if the fite fair takes two hours.* In our work with couples, this technique usually takes between an hour to an hour and a half.

The fite fair technique is best done with a counselor. However, if that is not possible, it can still work to allow venting to be done safely, providing the situation has not grown to unmanageable proportions. Attention has to be given to both's emotions regarding the subject about which each has previously "made" the other wrong. Through the fite fair, we explain to each other how we feel, how we see it in terms of the A/B Reality Tool, and what we want from the other person. It is an effective form of communication when the couple has reached an impasse.

At the end of a fite fair, it is important for the couple to embrace and celebrate the solution.

Sending and Receiving

One couple we know conducts discussions by telephone. When something important comes up she actually leaves the house and calls him from the car phone or from a pay phone. They've found what we've known—every statement made by one member of a couple needs a verbal response from the other. Ma Bell forces us to do that. Nonverbal responses or no-response responses cause inaccurate receipt of messages and often leave the speaker feeling unheard and unimportant.

Because we tend to hear things in the context of our own experience and from the perspective of our own gender, it is helpful to say back what we heard the other person say. Time and again people act on what they *think* the other said. Time and again, when we reexamine a conversation in the counseling office, the intent was entirely different from the way in which it was received.

"You said I was stupid to make that charge-card purchase!"

"Honey, I said we can't go on making charges, with the interest mounting up like it is."

Instructions. When your mate says something in an important conversation, say it back to him. *"What I heard you say was . . ."* If it wasn't accurate, simply ask him to say it again. A good phrase to use is just that: "Say again." Another phrase to use if the message is difficult to understand is, *"Help me understand. Say it another way."*

As you practice, you'll find that both of you will "get" the other's messages more and more accurately. You will also begin listening with more intent to hear just what the person said.

Calling a "Time Out"

Often when we discuss things with each other, one or the other wants to persist and pursue. The other may feel overwhelmed and start to fight or withdraw. Before either begins to yell or argue, it is helpful to call a "time out." This can be done with prearranged hand signals, perhaps the ones used by referees in football games, or with prearranged words—that stop the action.

When a time out is called it's a must to decide on another specific time when the discussion will be resumed. Make that date, and allow each other the time out.

Date Night

Following the first romantic stage of a relationship, couples get bogged down in the mundane. The first bloom diminishes, and many feel they have lost some of the intense love they shared.

Often, since the couple "fell in love" at one time, the qualities that led to the initial attraction are still there. With tenacity, time, and improved communication, that love can well be rekindled.

Instructions. The couple plans and keeps an evening out together every week. Understanding that this may be financially and logistically hard, the date is still prioritized into each week. The evening must be no briefer than three hours, and be spent on neutral ground. It cannot be at home. A public place like a restaurant modifies the intensity of tempers that might flare at home, and reduces distractions there. The time must be focused on the couple, so this isn't the time for a movie or an outing with another couple.

Chapter 7

SETTING UP A HOUSEHOLD

Should it be marriage—or will you live together? How will you tell your children? Where will you live? Who will make the decisions?

These are only a few of the questions that crop up when people choose to make a serious commitment and either live together or marry in step. For every question there is an answer that is unique for each stepfamily. Remember that there *are* remedies and resolutions. You have to take your time, assess your common goals, interests and vision of how things will be as partners in step. Make the time to do this work. It may save your relationship.

This may sound unromantic, and it may be contrary to your present romantic feelings. It should be. If you are going to be successful in step, you will have to look beyond the romance of the situation to the responsibilities. This approach should not be limited to relationships involving only single parents and their partners. It is a valuable approach to every relationship.

Living Together

Research indicates that the number of living-together couples with children has soared. In his 1994 research, Professor of Sociology Larry L. Bumpass of the University of Wisconsin states that *about one half of children under the age of thirteen* live in living-together step relationships. They live with one parent and that parent's partner, where the parent and partner are not married.

If you and your partner have chosen to live together, then you should be prepared to explain to your children why you have chosen living together over marriage. This is an important issue to children, for several reasons. Remember that a prior divorce or death has already left them distrustful. Mommy and Daddy were *married,* but the children are still left with only one full-time biological parent. How much security can they expect from an arrangement in which someone merely "lives with" their mother or father?

Another consideration that we may tend to overlook today, as the social rules and regulations have been stretched to the breaking point, is that children are very sensitive to their living arrangements. Living together in a large city may not pose any problem for the child both because of the impersonal nature of large urban areas and because the situation may be more common. However, not everyone lives in the big city.

School and other social institutions still operate according to traditional systems. In a living-together situation, your child may feel discomfort when family arrangements are referred to. Who should be addressed? Is it Mommy and Stepdaddy? Daddy and Stepmommy? Is it Mommy and Mommy's "friend"/"partner"/ whatever, and Daddy and Daddy's "friend"/"partner"/whatever?

Or, do you coach the child to refer to you as a single parent, with no mention of your live-in partner? This latter choice is dangerous, since it substantially devalues your partner's role in the home.

Unless you can help your child to feel comfortable with the living-together arrangement in the home, he will experience extreme discomfort outside of the home.

You have a special responsibility to the child in the living-together arrangement. One important area is determining how the child should relate to both the parent and the parent's lover. This can be difficult since the child has already had a bad experience with Mommy/Daddy, Male/Female roles.

The trauma and fear that the divorce may have touched off can be increased when the child sees that his parent is not marrying but only moving in with someone or having someone move in with them. This is the time to provide some honest and clear answers to your child's questions. You should also involve the child in the planning of the new household.

The decision to marry or to live together should not be based solely on the feelings of the child. Yet fairness requires that you take his/her feelings into account.

Whichever arrangement you choose, the same order must be extracted out of the madness that the step household can turn into. Rules must be established, and everyone in the household should know what is expected of him. It is easier to fit in when you know the place that you're supposed to fill.

Marriage or living together, the reactions of children will be strong. You are putting a new adult in their lives. Jealousy, resentment, defensive behavior, defiance, role confusion, and reaction to the new person may plague the child, who may be feeling torn. He may be overanxious to replace the parent figure. At the same time, he may pull away and act hostile because he feels loyalty to the absent parent.

In essence, in the stepfamily you have a group of people who all want to be loved, needed, and nurtured. They all have past memories with which to deal, and they all have a variety of loyalties that clash. Sorting their feelings out isn't easy. However, you do have to start somewhere.

It is at this point that the job descriptions you worked out in Chapter 6 will become valuable. Everybody should have a place in the new arrangement. From there, you can work on making the emotional connections that turn this arrangement into a stepfamily.

What is your role in the new household? What is your partner's role? What is the child's role? Defining the regulations and the household for the child and providing him with a clear view of what his place is within the new relationship are important. Children want security and structure. Letting a child know what is expected of him within the new family structure, as well as what he can expect, can be very comforting and reassuring to him.

Telling the Children

Telling the children is sometimes wonderful. They can be happy about having a new parent figure. Sometimes it's not so easy. Children can become frightened that instead of gaining a stepparent they are losing their natural parent. Adolescents, who are going through their own transitional stage and coping with hormones and emotions, may resent the intruder in their lives who will be taking away some of their influence in the natural parent's life. Older teens may experience competitive feelings with the newcomer, and sexual sparks may fly.

Even grown and married children may not make the telling easy. In addition to the emotional loyalties to the other parent and the unconscious fear of losing this parent to the new partner, they may begin to worry about how the marriage may affect their inheritance. Surely, for older children who have their own children, the remarriage complicates the grandparenting relationship.

Children of any age should know clearly that you love and

respect your new partner. You might gently begin to tell a young child in the following manner. "Tommy, you know that Jim has been spending a lot of time with us and that we do a lot of things together. I like having him with us all the time. Jim likes us very much, too, and he would like to be with us all the time." From that point, you can tell your child that you and Jim have decided to marry.

You should think carefully before talking to your child about the marriage. Be ready to provide answers to a lot of questions that are important to the child. "Where will we live?" "Where will Jim sleep?" "Will you still love me?" "Will Jim always live with us?" There may be many other questions, but they will all boil down to two: What will happen to me? How will our lives change?

No matter how much your child seemed to like having you date someone, viewing that man or that woman as a stepparent changes things quite a bit. Instead of an occasional visitor who exerts little influence on the child's day-to-day behavior and life, the stepparent will be a full-time occupant who will take away from the child's life with you. Your child may say it's fine but still be unconsciously afraid. He fears sharing your love, because he may lose you. What can he do? He is confused, and he needs a lot of assurance, guidance, and love.

Children need to be told in stages. They see you with a new partner. They are intuitive. They pick up your feelings with each other.

Should you be thinking about marriage or living together, usually children of most ages will already have asked you if you are going to marry.

Here is the opening for the pre-sell part of telling the children.

"What do you think, young lady, daughter darling?" Wait. They'll tell you. And they will often tell you a litany of concerns. Listen, assure. Sell the sizzle of the relationship for the child . . . and deliver it.

Children have legitimate concerns about their place and importance.

It is your job, with your partner, to have a vision of how the relationship will be good for all. The good news is you get more. The bad news is you get less.

The heart has many sections. It grows as we do. We will learn to care about respect, and even may love each other someday.

Yours, Mine, or *Ours*?

Once you've decided to create a joint household, you will have to decide where to live. Who moves in with whom? Or, does anybody move in with anybody else?

Often people who combine households will choose to move into the home of one of the partners. The reasons vary. Maybe one place is larger than the other. Sometimes the reason is that the children are settled in and moving would be just too much. Attachment to a home, the high cost of home and interest rates, the fact that the mortgage is paid off, or an ideal location are other ways in which people choose one home or the other.

While that might be initially convenient, it can provide the breeding ground for trouble in the stepfamily. Turf issues and the unwillingness to give up territory are only two of the reasons.

In *Living In Step* (McGraw-Hill, New York) written in 1976, we strongly urged a *new home* for a new family. Today this may be the making of financial difficulties. Costs are higher, interest rates are up, etc. If possible, do create a new home.

Here are some of the reasons: Somebody is going to feel like an outsider in another family's home. Everyone's home is filled with memories of the past. Living in your old home makes it too easy to continue thinking. "This is 'my' house and not 'our' house." You need to go from "mine" to "ours," and the home is an important part of that move.

Finding a new home together requires that both families get involved and join forces in the effort. It is not *her* home into which John and his kids are moving, nor are there protests as to whose room it "used to be before *this* (the marriage) happened."

Deciding upon and finding a new home together creates the opportunity for alignment within the new family. As you begin to look at which room should be Johnnie's and Johnnie says, "I want yellow walls," and you say—instead of "No"—"Well, maybe, let's see what color bedspreads you like," important interactions occur. We begin to discuss as husband and wife about the furniture. "I think that the brown chair should go there," the husband may say. The wife may disagree and tell him so: "No, the brown chair should go over here and a plant should go there."

Every item brought into the home that you've chosen as a family, whether it is an apartment or a house, brings you closer together as a family. Deciding what comes into the home and where even the smallest item should go requires problem solving. Problem solving together generates bonding together.

Together, the parent and stepparent listen to what the children say that they want. The children don't run the family, but you should give them feedback on what they think. Make choices, but leave some for the children. They may choose between yellow or blue or green or tan for their rooms. The family, biological children, stepchildren, and both parents, can share points of view for the shared rooms.

Together you begin to align. "Oh, I think that the kitchen's got to be yellow, with that yellow wallpaper." "No, I like the blue and white." Together, as a family, you begin to solve problems. Together, as husband and wife, you begin to become familiar with each other's tastes.

Look over magazines together before starting your new home and discuss the pictures in the magazines rather than argue over an actual new home with your new family. If there are going to be some deep arguments about your tastes in living quarters, this is a good way to begin developing family cohesion. Get those arguments and disagreements out into the open. It helps to build the relationship.

Now, what if a new home (house or apartment) and new furniture is financially out of your reach? That is a very strong possibility. When this is the case, the new stepfamily should work on creating a new home out of their joint possessions. While the premises might remain the old home base of one part of the family, the furnishings and decorating taste should become an expression of all of the people who now make up the family.

In most cases, not all of the furniture of both families can be squeezed into the one home. Therefore, *both* families will have to give up something so that their lives and goods can be combined. The sorting out and selection process can be a time of interacting. Everybody helps in the decision-making process. Furniture should be rearranged. Rooms should be repainted. Wallpaper may be chosen. The new family can create a home that will become the family home, in which all members can feel that they belong.

Once you've decided on your step relationship, told the children, and set up your new home, your life as a stepfamily has begun.

Chapter 8

GETTING ORGANIZED

Simply saying "I do" and moving into the same home will not make your stepfamily fall immediately into place. As you already know from earlier discussions, there is a lot of sorting out of the human relationships to be done *before* you move in together.

Who Am I Anyway?

Roles have to be identified. Responsibilities have to be assigned. Everyone has to know where he fits in. The rules and regulations of the family have to be established.

Remember the debugging exercises you did in Chapter 6? That wasn't just busywork. These tools—the Notion of the Family, the Time/Energy/Money Grid and the Job Descriptions—help to sort out your thinking. They don't, however, provide all of the answers. Even the most carefully prepared adults in step soon find that they have to make up some of the answers as they go along.

There are no safe patterns to follow. No instructions which, if followed to the letter, will guarantee success.

Even if there are no sure patterns, you can rely on certain guidelines to help you through the process of becoming a family. The house rules should be clear to everyone, and everyone should be expected to abide by the rules. Consequences for violating rules and standards should be clearly stated in advance and known by the children. Everybody should know what is expected of him by other members of the stepfamily. Everyone should have a firmly established role in the home. Such guidelines can give all stepfamily members a feeling of security.

What is your place in the stepfamily? Your partner's? The children's?

Are you the father? The *step*father? Or both?

Are you the mother? The *step*mother? Or both?

Are you the oldest, middle, or youngest child? The oldest, middle, or youngest *step*child?

Are you, perhaps, confused? The step situation does lead you to count the possibilities in relationships. John may be the stepfather in the stepfamily that is comprised of Sally and her two boys. However, when his own daughter visits, he assumes the role of father to her while remaining the stepfather for Sally's sons.

John's daughter, in turn, is both John's daughter and Sally's stepdaughter for the time that she is in John and Sally's home. Also during the time that John's daughter is visiting, Sally must function as both mother to her sons and as stepmother. Her sons are both full-time children in the home and full-time stepchildren.

The interrelationships become even more involved when two people having children move in together, bringing with them their children and their dual roles of biological and step to all relationships. Thus, while the adults are each Mommy and Daddy to their own children, they become *step*mommy and *step*daddy to each other's children. The children also experience this dual role, and the differing responses that result.

You can hardly tell the participants and their roles without a scorecard. You, however, have the key to that scorecard if you take the time to debug the relationship before your step relationship becomes a stepfamily. Your probing may create hostility and anger, but such feelings are easier to deal with before the serious commitment is made. When handled afterwards, they are often more emotionally charged and more difficult to resolve.

Discipline and Structure

"Don't you touch my son!" Is that what you think of when your attention moves to discipline in the stepfamily? Well, that's part of it. Discipline in the stepfamily can be a very difficult issue. Everyone has a different view of how, when, and why you discipline.

What is discipline? It doesn't mean blind obedience. *Webster's New Collegiate Dictionary* defines discipline as: 1) instruction; 2) a subject that is taught; 3) training that corrects, molds, or perfects; 4) orderly or prescribed conduct or pattern of behavior.

It is not just punishment. Discipline is simply a way of training children and ourselves to act in an orderly fashion. It is a more specific area of the overall structuring of a household. You, as a member of the household, are expected to act in a certain way and to do certain things. The same is expected of the children.

You discipline by establishing standards of behavior and by setting limits. When these standards of behavior and limits are violated, then the children must accept the consequences. Before you can begin to discipline, you have to know the results you want.

Don't expect your children to play your game if you haven't set the rules for them, or if you keep changing the rules. You may have already assigned them their tasks and listed the consequences for not performing their tasks, but is that discipline? Well, it is if you take the time and expend the effort to see that the tasks are done, and, if they are not done, enforce the consequences.

Are there certain types of behavior that you don't and do want in your home? Discuss this with all the children *before* an incident occurs, so that you can also discuss the consequences of such behavior. In this way, you, your children, and your stepchildren know when a rule has been broken and when consequences will happen.

The parents, not the children, are responsible for structuring the family and for realigning the relationships among family members. It is the parent and stepparent who introduce a new set of procedures, techniques, and how-tos into the new family. No matter what everyone else did in their old, pre-step families, this is the way you do it now. Whether the children are visiting or living with you on a full-time basis, you have to make it clear that the structure of the new family has to be followed.

If you're told by a visiting child that "Mom doesn't make me do this at home," you have every right to respond that "in this home, we do it this way, so that is what you'll be doing in this house."

Household Duties and Responsibilities

In structuring the family, every member of the family should be given jobs, no matter what their age. The days of hired help are, for the most part, gone so most family members expect to have regular duties. The stepfather or stepmother is not the maid or servant in the household, as all too often is the case. As parents, you should sit down and carefully determine the jobs that need to be done. Then assign those jobs. For example, some of the family will handle pre-meal procedures, others will maintain the bathroom, an older child may take care of the car, and all members should keep their own rooms neat. Even very young children will enjoy being assigned tasks that let them know that they are important in keeping the household running smoothly.

Plan carefully and make certain that everyone in the household knows their role.

Assigning Tasks

1. List the duties and the responsibilities of each household member.

2. Set deadlines for the completion of duties.

3. State clearly the consequences of *not* completing assigned duties and the positive consequences of doing the tasks.

Structuring the household applies even to children who come for visitation. Children, even older children, want to know what is expected of them. "Can I help with the dishes?" or "I see that you're making a salad . . . can I chop something?" You need to bring them into the circle by letting them be part of activities.

Certainly, there is a very practical side to taking the time to structure your household carefully. Many people in step relationships are overworked at home. Spreading the work around takes care of this problem.

You and your partner may have some problem in deciding where the jobs lie. Or, you may be so used to doing everything yourself that delegating responsibility can be difficult. Don't worry. Once you have begun to share the work, you'll find that a team effort will emerge. Not only will the work be done, but it will be done as a family.

Deciding the Jobs

1. Take a walk through each room of your home and outside of the house.

2. Look at the garage, the car, the lawn, the walk.

3. Write down those jobs that need to be done.

4. Consider the ages of the children and, together, decide who will do each of the jobs.

Certainly, little children can't do that much, but they can be very helpful in setting the table, clearing the table, emptying the garbage, and running various errands. Both parents should create these lists and decide the assignment of responsibilities. Once you and your partner have come to an agreement, then you should jointly tell the children what you have decided.

They may have their own preferences, and you can listen to their feedback. In the long run, however, the children should not decide. That's your job.

You should also have a list of consequences ready that will be applied if the jobs and responsibilities are not handled properly. Here the children can collaborate. Ask them what the consequences should be if they don't get things done. Will it be two hours of no TV on Saturday night? Should they be grounded for half a day on Sunday? Should their allowance be delayed (but not withheld)?

Negotiate the consequences. Decide in advance with the children what the consequences for neglecting their duties will be, as well as the positive consequences for completing their duties. Extra-good behavior gets extra-good consequences. Post the list where children can see it. The refrigerator is a handy place. We all need to know what is expected of us, and this is especially true of children in step. The point is to create a win-win situation, set a precedent, and end frustration for all of you.

How To Discipline

We recommend, at least initially, that biological parents should discipline their own children. Children tend to forgive their biological parents for a wide variety of actions that they don't accept willingly from a stepparent. The relationship has existed for a longer time, and there is also the blood link to consider. In addition, step already has a bad press.

While a child may resent the stepparent's applying consequences to his behavior, he may think differently when it is his biological parent who is pulling in the reins. "That's my mother who is taking away my TV time. I'm going to love her anyway, even if I can't watch TV, because the leaves were supposed to be raked by four o'clock and it's now seven."

That doesn't mean that the stepparent has to stand by helplessly while the children do what they want. What it does mean is that both parents must be united in their efforts at discipline and at enforcing the consequences. Once you have determined the role and responsibility of each child, once the standards for behavior in the home are set, *there should be no confusion as to what is expected* of them.

Discipline When The Biological Parent Is Not Home

As a rule, the biological parent disciplines. Should he or she not be there when a violation of the house rules occurs, the child is reminded of the rules and asked to comply. Should the stepparent feel that he/she can get compliance at the time, he/she should ask for it. If not, he/she should remind the child and discuss the incident with the biological parent.

Parents and stepparents need to be consistent in enforcing discipline to keep the stepfamily running smoothly. Even visiting children are not excused from the rules of the house. This, in the beginning, can be a sensitive issue.

In some cases, the visiting child will test the strength of the discipline by saying, "But, I always stay up late on weekends at home." You may answer, "In this house, the rules are different."

Chapter 9

COUPLE STRENGTH

The couple in step has the main responsibility for making the step relationship work. Adults must assess their roles, define their roles and those of the children in the relationship, define discipline for their household and apply the consequences, identify and create rituals, and provide the step etiquette for the family.

In addition, the couple must make the time to nurture the love that brought them together. With all that they have to do, and because of the conflicts that emerge as a result of the opposing pulls of sexual and blood energy that each may experience, as a couple in step they may feel like they are constantly under fire. The most effective way to overcome these difficulties is to confront the step situation *together*.

Couple strength is primary. The stepfamily can't function without it. However, unless you have discussed your expectations with each other, neither of you will know what it is that you are supposed to do. Many couples simply assume: "you are a woman, so you do the mothering." "You are a man, so you do the fathering." In step, it isn't that simple.

Flip back to the measures to which you responded in Chapter 6. Look at the Notion of the Family measure. What is your notion of the family? What is your partner's notion? Can you bring the two notions together?

Have you examined your responses to the Time/Energy/Money Grid? Where are the areas of agreement? Where are the areas of contention? How can you compromise and build up your couple strength?

Review your job descriptions for the family. How do you meet your partner's expectations for your role? Where are the areas in which you can compromise?

The Instant Parent

Becoming an instant parent is hard for both men and women. One week you are sleeping late, reading the papers in bed and running your own life. The next week you are trying to hold your own in a family that has long-established rhythms, patterns, and emotional ties.

The shock can be great. No matter how fully you were aware that your partner was a parent and that living together or marriage would mean becoming an instant parent, the reality always seems to be more than you bargained for.

Suddenly, the friendly greetings of the children may turn to sullen stares. Your partner will have to share his/her attention with the children. You will find yourself vying for attention with the children who may barely acknowledge your existence. Don't be surprised if the question "Is it worth it?" begins to dominate your thinking.

You are used to shopping, going out with friends, stopping for a drink, or doing any other of a hundred things *when* you want to. Once you are an instant parent, the spontaneity is tamed.

Your money was your own, to spend however frivolously you

pleased. New clothes? Jewelry? A car? Plays? You name it. Now, you may very well find that your money has become their money, too. You may be helping to support your stepchildren. You may be contributing money to the home because your spouse is supporting his prior family. You may even begin to feel that you were only married for your paycheck.

You may be treated like a substitute teacher sometimes, no matter how strong your relationship with the children may have been before the marriage. The children may be jealous of you and distrustful of your new power in their lives. They may try some nasty tricks to get back to their old relationship with their parent. You are not their parent, and most children want their old family back.

You may find that, however talented, handsome, beautiful, and warm-hearted the children may have found you before, marriage to their parent will immediately turn you into the stereotype of the cruel stepfather or cruel stepmother. Try to be a compassionate listener, and the stepchildren may tag you as nosy. Ask to take them someplace, and the stepchildren may say that you are bothering them. Offer to help them with a project, and you may be accused of always butting in.

If your partner is a noncustodial parent, then you will become a parent only on weekends or at other specified times. Here, in addition to trying to establish a relationship with the children, you may find yourself saddled with them when your spouse must be away on business, or even playing tennis. Thus, the stepparent may become an unwelcome companion to unhappy stepchildren during visitation.

On the other hand, as the parent you may find your partner chooses to pursue his/her own life and participate only minimally in the visitation. Without previous agreement this will only create resentment on your part.

As a couple, it's vital to clarify our expectations about each other's children. Resentments and hurts about this can severely erode the couple strength.

The number one problem with which people come to our counselors at the Stepfamily Foundation is: "We love each other, but our individual relations with one or the other's children is assaulting this relationship."

Remember that as the instant parent you entered an established family. You are an alien being in the body of the family. It will take time for the new stepfamily fully to integrate patterns of living, loving, and feeling. For a long time, you may find that your accomplishments will be compared to Mom's or Dad's—and you will lose by contrast. Of course, the kids won't even ask you about what you do. But when you and your partner structure the family and devise a step etiquette and discipline for the family, an orderly period of adjustment will evolve.

The Single Parent

The instant parent often marries the single parent who may have had an independent life with the children for a number of years. They have developed a pattern that already has a niche in it for everyone in the family—except for the instant parent.

Raising children, working for a living, keeping the house going and doing all the things that two parents do, but on the energy of only one, the single parent develops a variety of strengths. The family has become a unit that has shown itself able to survive, in spite of the odds.

Into their lives comes someone who loves their mother or father and who innocently supposes that the single parent is tired of all of that responsibility. Another adult can take off some of the financial burden, provide greater guidance for the children, assist in the home, and provide emotional support. The single parent may agree, in theory.

Once the two are married, however, everybody's perception appears to change. The single parent resents giving up responsibility, fails to consult with the spouse in decisions, and prefers to remain the sole parent figure in the home. The new spouse feels devalued and feels like an outsider in his own home.

Can anything be done? Yes, if the adults love each other and want the relationship to work. They will have to examine their views of the family, delegate responsibilities to each other and to the children, and jointly provide the structure that gives everyone a place in the family.

Being Stepparents to Each Other's Children

When two parents marry, they automatically become stepparents to each other's children. Such a situation is volatile, since it brings together two single parents, assorted children, and the need to establish a home base, which may be the home of one of the families. What to do when this happens was discussed in Chapter 5.

Once again, even though both people are parents and they presumably know how to deal with the children, neither has experience with *step*children. For many parents, seeing their children turn into "wicked" stepchildren in the eyes of their lover is a gruesome surprise. Her children resent him. His children resent her. The children from one family resent the children from the other family.

The adults must establish step couple control. Structuring the family is a start toward overcoming the complexities of step. It is the responsibility of the couple.

Putting the Couple First

The step situation can produce some very heavy-duty issues that must fall on the shoulders of the couple. Adults make the rules and set the consequences for breaking the rules. It is not healthy for children to run the marriage or to dominate the household. Check, stop, look. Make sure who's in charge. Lovingly, as a couple, envision how you wish to and will run your household.

Many couples need to seek outside counseling. At the Stepfamily Foundation it takes an average of ten to fifteen sessions to teach that couple strength. Counseling in step is time well spent.

A major problem of most couples who marry into step is that they concentrate on the parenting roles, and they forget to nurture themselves as a couple. Couple time, time alone, is often pushed aside.

It is damaging to the relationship. We need to nurture the relationship just as much as we need to nurture the children. In many cases, when the couple begins to pay more attention to the couple relationship, problems in the rest of the family begin to lessen, because the couple forms a unified front that aids in motivating the children to comply with the newly established structures.

When you are dating, you are anxious and adamant about helping each other. You are in love and adore each other. You can't get enough of each other's company.

Once you marry or move in together, however, the daily responsibilities can overwhelm and drive a wedge between the two of you.

For the sake of each other and for your family, take one night a week to spend completely alone. Beg, borrow, or bribe a family member to babysit for you, have older children in the family babysit, or hire a babysitter. Get away to where you can talk and enjoy each other's company just as you did when you dated. Talk, but not about step, the state of the marriage, or the children. Talk about movies, the news, music, pottery, anything.

Ten Steps for Steps

Keep in mind the Ten Steps for Steps. Keep them handy and refer to them when some of the totally expected problems of step appear unexpectedly.

1. Recognize that the stepfamily will not and can not function as does a natural family.
2. Recognize the hard fact that the children are not yours and they never will be.
3. Super stepparenting doesn't work.
4. Discipline styles must be sorted out by the couple.
5. Establish clear job descriptions between the parent and stepparent and the respective children.
6. Know that unrealistic expectations beget rejections and resentments.
7. There are no ex-parents . . . only ex-spouses.
8. Be prepared for the conflicting pulls of sexual and biological energies within the step relationship.
9. The conflict of loyalties must be recognized right from the beginning.
10. Guard your sense of humor, and use it.

Classic Differences between Step and Biological Responses to Children

Before we become stepparents and parents in the step household, it is important to notice how differently interactions are perceived. What is normal and handleable and even lovable in the intact household may become a gigantic upset in step. What follows are two examples of a young girl's budding sexuality and a natural desire to be "daddy's girl," played out in an intact situation and in a step situation.

Pubescent Girl and Daddy

Eva was nubile, darling, and becoming quite beautiful. She was just turning twelve. She was beginning to find her womanhood and was trying it out on Daddy.

In an intact family the scene would play this way:

Eva always came down to breakfast in some form of tee shirt or sweat shirt. One sunny spring morning, she came down in one of Mommy's nightgowns, one budding breast partially visible. She smiled at Daddy. A different little smile this day. Coy, charming, and sexy, as only a little twelve-year-old girl can be. Today she is moving in differently. Gone are the girlish ways—she slides her chair close to Daddy's. He looks slightly embarrassed, but amused. The mother and father give each other one of those looks: See how our daughter is growing up. Both smile, knowing she is going to be a beauty. Dad notes to Mom that she is going to have some body, too.

Then, usually, Mom goes ahead and begins to set things straight. She may put her arm around Dad indicating: Hey dear daughter, this is my man. You will find yourself another. And it's over. Normal. Handled and over.

Now imagine the same scene in a step situation.

Pubescent girl is visiting Dad and stepmom for a month in the summer. Same scene occurs. Dad has really been looking forward to seeing his little girl. Dad bashfully ignores or responds sweetly to her advances.

Stepmom tells the girl to go upstairs and put on a bathrobe.

There is a bite of harshness in her voice. The girl sulks off to her room, leaving Dad and stepmom alone at the breakfast table. Dad and stepmom have a fight . . . or don't talk to each other at all, each blaming the other. Pubescent daughter ends up in tears and says she is going home to her Mom.

In step territory, turf and sexuality may invade every corner of our transactions. These invasions come in forms alien to those of the intact family.

Here is the classic Daughter in the Front Seat scenario:

Daddy goes in to pick up his little girl. She immediately scrambles to the front seat of the car in between Daddy and Sara. Daddy puts his arm around the little girl. He doesn't tell her to get in the back of the car. And Daddy and his little girl hug and are close. Sara fumes. How dare she? How dare *he?* And what's wrong with me?

What to do? Daddy may not dare to expect that the lady in his life will feel or act like a mother, or even a sister. He needs to recognize that he is in the middle here. The play is a delicate one. The goal is to give *both* daughter and lady enough self-confidence in him so they don't feel left out and unloved. He is in the middle and he needs to give them enough self-esteem to enable them to handle these often unpredictable, upsetting, and endemic situations that crop up in step. No easy task.

In addition, he must set the boundaries for his daughter. "No little one, you will sit in the back. Off my lap sweetie, I must drive, and Sara sits in the front. Grownups in the front. Children in the back. That's my young lady."

Sara needs to hold her fury. If Dad, her man, does these things . . . without even seeing what's going on . . . Sara needs to know this kind of behavior is part of step.

The Woman Who Has Never Parented

One of the most important populations we deal with at the Stepfamily Foundation is *women who have never parented.* Often these women must deal with children only a few years younger than themselves. So we have written a special set of Ten Steps for the Woman Who Has Never Parented.

1. Competition often occurs between a new love and his children. You may feel that you are directly competing with them. You may be . . . *but you don't have to.*

2. Recognize that he has had many more years playing father to them than lover to you. You may have to make allowances, give him time. *Remember,* however, there are limits. Counseling may enable you realistically to define them.

3. Usually he feels that he has not had enough time with his children and feels the need to catch up when they are together. Guilt may be a motivating factor. But discuss and agree on expectations about time spent with you and time spent with his children.

4. You may feel that his girls come on to him sexually. He may not notice. What is "cute" to the biological father and mother may not be perceived as such by you. Competition between daughter and his woman can be strong. Whose man is he, anyway? You can often gain ground by giving them time together and gently clarifying with him what is sexual and what is affectionate behavior.

5. Establish clear job descriptions between the parent and stepparent and the children. What specifically is the job of each one of us in this household? We need to be specific.

6. The sexual bonds between you and your man may come into conflict with the biological bonds between him and his children. The conflicting pulls of sexual and biological energies within the step relationship can polarize the family.

7. Sort out how discipline is handled. The couple should agree on discipline styles.

8. The natural parent generally should discipline.

9. Blame for problems that are unique to the step relationship is often misplaced. We tend to blame others and ourselves, failing to recognize the problems as inherent in the step relationship.

10. Guard your sense of humor, and use it.

Chapter 10

THE CHILDREN OF STEP

My Mom says
My Dad is "No Good."
My Dad says
My Mom is "No Good."
I say
I'm "No Good."
And I am probably right. . . .

Donny: A Child's World Is His Family

Donny would run along with both parents, each arm reaching
high—one to Mommy, one to Daddy. Then one, two, three,
swwwiinnnngggg, Donny would swoop through the air. "Again!
Again!" he'd shout. One, two, threee. . . .

Sometimes they'd go to the beach. Daddy would take him out
in the water and hold him tight while the waves rolled around
them. He'd laugh while the white water smashed around Daddy

and him. Nothing bad could happen when Daddy was there. Back to the blanket where Mommy would have lunch, sandwiches, and cold drinks. Before they packed up to leave, Mommy and Daddy would swing him in the blanket, one on each side, and toss him in the air. Whoowee!

It was all warm and happy. Mommy laughed a lot. Daddy would come home early and play bear on the rug, grumbling bear noises and rubbing him with his prickly whiskers. Daddy could do everything and would show him how.

There came the time, then, when Mommy stopped laughing and Daddy stopped coming home early. Bear! Bear! he'd shout, but Daddy and Mommy weren't hearing him.

In the night he'd wake up scared. He'd dream that Mommy and Daddy were fighting. But still the voices went on. The dream wasn't over. "Daddy! Daddy! Mommy! Mommy! daddymommydaddymommydaddymommydaddy!"

"There, there." They would both rush into the room and stroke him and hold him tight. Bad dream! There, there, the little boy's all right. Clutching something furry in his little fist, he'd go back to sleep.

Then one afternoon, he heard them fighting in the next room. Low voices getting louder and softer, all tough and edgy like sandpaper. He couldn't move; he stood there listening, holding his breath. Clear as a cannon, he heard Daddy: "How can you ask me to give up that wonderful boy?"

The world stopped, and somewhere in the void he heard the word "Divorce! divorce! divorce!" crashing like so many waves of disaster. He'd never heard it before, he didn't know what it meant, but he knew it was horrible.

He was staring at his toy chest with the circus animals, red and yellow, marching bravely around it. Time stopped. The next thing he knew, Mommy and Daddy, together, were both holding him, and he heard himself shrieking a high-pitched, tearing scream.

The Loss

A child's world is his family. When that breaks, his sense of self and his security are shattered. Most children in one way or another have been held up by both parents. Mother and father on either side hold a hand and swing the child over the rough spots as over the curb. When one of them leaves, the child is yanked out of proportion. Now he's supported on one side, and the other side is left hanging.

Living in Step
McGraw Hill, 1977

This was written in 1975. Today the story holds true even more poignantly—except that children today expect and even anticipate that their parents will get divorced. It is also expected of children that they handle divorce with acceptance. Millions of children, we feel, carry with them, at some level, a burden of deepseated, very often unconscious resentment concerning the safety of their lives within the family. Indeed they should, since we have not provided them with a secure environment in which to grow up.

Vance Packard, in *Our Endangered Children* (Little, Brown, Boston), addresses what he calls a national problem. He documents a vital but as yet undiscussed issue: "America has unwittingly developed an antichild culture." Packard describes today's society from the point of view of its negative impact on children, focusing on the important changes of the last twenty years—the spiraling divorce rate, the women's movement, and the fact that over 50 percent of women work away from home.

The women's movement resulted in the introduction of millions of women into the work force, including 80 percent of mothers and 90 percent of stepmothers. This fact is also the result of an economy marked by downward mobility, mandating many women's employment as an economic necessity.

It's important to look at the statistics once again. Only 5.7 percent of the 83,500,000 households in the U.S. consist of the nuclear family in that there is a working father, a homemaking mother, and two or more children. Women today receive greater rewards for career development than they do for effective parenting or the development of a family. The skills of the marketplace receive far more attention than the skills of parenting. This phenomenon results not only in many women's choosing not to have children but also in our children's having fewer and fewer resource people available to them.

This is further exacerbated by the exclusionary and often unstable dynamics of stepfamilies and remarriages. Again the numbers speak clearly. It is predicted that by the year 2000 the average American family will be a stepfamily. At the Stepfamily Foundation, our research indicates that the average American relationship, whether dating, single parent, living together, or remarriage, is already a step relationship. In these numbers we have included only heterosexual relationships. Homosexuals who have children experience the same step dynamics when they live with or visit their biological children. Not even twenty years ago most children had at least two and often four people who focused their main attention on them. Today's child is indeed fortunate to have one fulltime person concerned with his well-being.

Kids in Step: Common Complaints

- I want my old family back. I want things the way they were, I miss things the way they were—even though Mom and Dad fought.
- Nobody has enough time for me.
- I'm sad when Mom's sad, and I'm sad when Dad's sad, and they are both sad too much.
- I don't know what they want from me.
- I'm angry and don't know why.
- Dad is busy with his new family.

- It's boring over at Dad's house.
- It's wonderful at Dad's house. I wish I could live with Dad.
- I miss my father.
- Dad and I have a great time, except for "her."
- He gives more to her kids and to her than us.
- He never thought about us when he moved.
- Dad left Mom, but he really left me.
- There must be something wrong with me.
- Mom is wonderful, but that friend of hers is awful.
- She's always paying attention to him and not us.
- She lets him tell us what to do.
- They go away together and leave us alone.
- She has always done things for me, and now he says she spoils me.
- She lets him say awful things about me.
- I don't want to say hello to him.
- I wish he weren't here.
- We've been doing just fine without him. Why do we need him now?
- It's not fair. . . .
- I don't know where I belong.
- They will never know how hard it is to visit Dad/Mom.
- They get upset when I tell them about the good time I had when I visit.
- Mom doesn't have enough money. I wish I could help her out.
- Dad doesn't know how hard it is at home without him. A woman in step is not . . .
- My mother (or my brother's mother, my sister's mother, the dog's mother, etc.).
- The boss in this house! (Everyone knows Daddy is—except Daddy!)
- Fair! (She picks on all of us because she is not our mother—how's that for a catch 22!)

- As good a cook as Mommy. (Meanwhile, is anyone volunteering for kitchen duty?)
- Pretty. (Heaven forbid, everyone knows God and stepchildren don't love "ugly"—the other side of "mean.")
- Even my stepmother. (That's Daddy's girlfriend—the kids never saw her before.)

Do these complaints sound familiar? As part of a step situation, you most likely have at least a dozen more to add to this list.

The most important, yet most frequently unspoken, complaint of children in a step situation is that they don't like the changes that divorce and remarriage of their parents have brought into their lives. Most of the time, whatever else they may say, they are really saying, "I want my old family back . . . I miss things the way they were . . . even if Dad and Mom fight."

That desire is the hardest for children to articulate because it appears to go against everything that the adults want. Faced with no other way of showing their feelings, children in step act out, behave badly, act disrespectful and seem to be indifferent to life. "I don't know" and "I don't care" punctuate their conversation and their thinking. What that translates to is: I care so much, I don't dare to care. I cared in the past . . . I was hurt . . . I'll show 'em . . . if I don't care . . . they can't hurt me. Their behavior may drive their parents and stepparents nuts. Most often the children of step are crying for attention, love, and a family they can count on, one that is predictable. They need help in dealing with all the frightening changes that have invaded their lives. You can help.

Grief

Many of the children of step relationships don't function in the same way as adored, comfortable, loved children from biological homes. When parents divorce or a parent dies, children suffer a destructive loss in their lives. They may seem rude or unruly, but they are really terrified. They act out, but don't know why. They can't find the words to name the fear.

The more grief they are feeling, the more children will give grief to the adults in their lives. Children act bad because they feel bad. Children (and adults, too) have to get control, because they fear the loss of control. Many children feel if they had only "done something," the family would still be together. Like someone caught in the grip of an unknown presence, many of the children of step are fighting unnamable internal monsters.

The Damage to Children After Divorce

Judith Wallerstein, Ph.D. is the most prominent researcher of divorce and its impact on children in the U.S. In her landmark study, she found that only 45 percent of children do well after divorce; 41 percent are doing poorly, worried, underachieving, deprecating, and often angry; 14 percent are strikingly uneven, too soon to say how they would turn out.

Forty percent of the nineteen-to-twenty-three-year-old young men had no goals, a limited education, and a sense of having no control of their lives. Thirty-three percent of girls between nineteen and twenty-three—who previously seemed to be unimpaired by the divorce—suffered what was labeled as the "sleeper effect." As soon as they experience their first serious relationship they leave it for fear it will not work.

Sixty percent of children felt rejection by one of their parents, usually the father. Fourteen percent saw both their father and their mother happily remarried after ten years. Fifteen percent saw their mother or father undergo a second divorce.

According to Wallerstein, "Divorce is the single most important cause of enduring pain in the adolescent's life."

We are in complete in agreement with her figures, as they seem to have been borne out by our work with divorced families since 1975.

The new families being formed today by these children as they reach adulthood are particularly vulnerable to demise. When a marriage breaks down both sexes experience a diminished capacity to parent, according to Dr. Wallerstein.

As we have stated before, divorced parents provide less time, less discipline, and are less sensitive to the children as they are caught up in their own divorce and its aftermath. Many parents focus more on themselves than on their children. In essence they are caught up with their own lives and parenting takes on a lesser value. As diminished parenting continues, it permanently disrupts childrearing.

These parents often do not guide their children. As a result, the children's role often becomes self-determined and parental in itself, as the child helps the parent to ward off depression.

One might conclude that parents become more childlike and helpless and children become more of the center of the family and more self-regulating. The child's psychological condition relates directly to the post-divorce quality of life.

Wallerstein states that "Young people said time and time again how much they needed family structure and clear guidelines. An alarming number felt abandoned both physically and emotionally."

Wallerstein's findings on school work include:

- Children from intact homes do better on fourteen of sixteen classroom behavior ratings: social adjustment (popularity, ability to communicate, getting along with others) and school work (higher I.Q.s, better grades, greater self-discipline).
- 30 percent of children from two-parent homes are high achievers.
- 1 percent of children from one-parent homes are high achievers.

- 1 percent of children from two-parent homes are low achievers.
- 40 percent of children from one-parent homes are low achievers.
- Girls consistently adjust better and faster than boys do, both socially and academically—implying that boys may be suffering more from the absence of their fathers.

And, we have not begun to deal with the effects of re-divorce!

The good news is that if you follow our guidelines and structure you will not become one of these ugly statistics. Single parents *can* do a good job; you just have to parent very actively.

How Children React

A step relationship only exists if one or both of the partners has children. Children make the step relationship. They have also been blamed for the breakup of many such relationships.

At the Stepfamily Foundation, we often hear this plaintive cry from parents: "The children are pulling our relationship apart!" The statement denotes helplessness. But it is helplessness on the part of the adults. They give children trauma and power that children are not prepared to handle, then blame them for upsets within the relationship. And then the children *do* cause the upsets. They need structure, guidance, and rules, which are supposed to be supplied by the adults—their parents and stepparents.

Children want the intact home back. They show us this in their behavior toward the new people who enter our lives. They may be rude, act fresh, ignore us, or berate us. All in all, they make us miserable.

Yet who created these feelings? It doesn't matter. What *does* matter is that you and your partner know that children in step situations are not being vicious or vindictive. They are just acting on their fears. Children, as well as adults, will constantly defend what they believe to be their territory. They will fight to regain what they feel they have lost.

Some children will not be so direct in their feelings. Divorce and the dating parent may result in a child who may be almost too good to be true. He is quiet, polite, always helpful and accommodating. Mommy or Daddy praise him as the "little angel" who is such a comfort. That is a child who may be more in need of attention than the squeaky wheel who gives us so much trouble.

The too-good child may be feeling even more conflict than his peers who act out. He, too, wants life to be the same as it was before, and he may really want Mommy or Daddy to marry *somebody,* just so that he can have a whole family again. Even though he also feels loss, fear, concern, and the host of other emotions that the acting out child exhibits, the too-good child represses these feelings. He lives, in effect, a dual life.

He is afraid to be disruptive, because he may drive away both the remaining parent and any potential Daddies or Mommies. And he also feels a sense of disloyalty to the parent who isn't present. At the same time, he may feel abandoned by the parent who isn't present, and his self-esteem is suffering mightily.

If your child appears to be almost too good and too well-behaved for his age, he just may be. Children who have experienced the trauma of divorce or death, and who have had to cope with great changes in their lives, should be expected to have needs that we must meet. They should be expected to show fear, anger, and distress. When they don't they are carrying their burdens alone. That isn't fair.

You and Your Children in Step

Children need structure. Children need discipline. Discipline equals love and guidance. Children need to have an awareness of the etiquette of the step household. Children need to know where they fit in and what is expected of them. These ideas pervade this book and they underlie the whole plan of making a success of the step relationship.

The child who was the oldest in the prior family may become the middle child or the youngest in the stepfamily. The child who was Mommy's or Daddy's main emotional support during the period of divorce and through the difficult pre-step years will find himself being replaced by a newcomer adult. The child who was the center of attention in the single parent family will find that he may now take second or third place in his parent's attentions.

Wouldn't we all act out if we found our position in life so drastically changed?

Wouldn't we "hate" the person responsible for our demotion? How "real" would we feel?

Parents and stepparents have to step back from their own troubles when the step situation becomes difficult and place themselves in the position of the children. Wouldn't we like to know the rules, so that we can decide whether we will follow them or try to break them?

Most adults would. Well, so do children. You have to draw up the family plan and see that everyone in the family knows what it is. Go back to the measures in Chapter 6. Become fully aware of what your job descriptions for the children are before you begin to impose rules and discipline in the home. Both the parent and stepparent have to work as a unit so that the children will understand that these rules are for the *family,* and that they are firm.

Aids for Helping Your Children

1. *Talk with the children.* Issues such as disloyalty, family role, interpersonal feelings, and the like have to be brought out into the open.

2. *Let the children know that they don't have to feign or feel love for the stepparent.* It should not be expected of them. Common courtesy and respect will do at the outset.

3. *Let children know that they should not feel distressed if the stepparent does not feign or appear to feel love for them.* It's just too much to ask of a group of people who have *created* a family, not evolved one.

4. *Let the children know where they stand in the family.* Tell them their duties and expected behavior. Set the positive consequences for achieving duties, rules, jobs, and the negative consequences for failing to perform duties or for misbehavior.

5. Hold weekly family meetings. Build a team.

6. But, remember, *you* are the team captains—the male and female heads of the household.

7. Develop planned and scheduled activity times.

8. Be sympathetic around visitation. Remember that it isn't easy for anyone involved.

9. When children act out, misbehave, or seek control for apparently no reason, see if you can find out what's really going on.

10. Maintain respectful behavior between you as a couple in front of the children. The children should not be able to get the couple upset with each other.

The burden appears to be on the adult in the stepfamily, and it is, for the most part. Yet, there are many contributions that children can make to the relationship. Coming from their positions of loss, fear, and disillusionment, it is difficult at first for children in step to recognize the favorable aspects of their lives. As adults, both parents and stepparents, it is our role, and more, our *responsibility* to our children, our stepfamilies, and ourselves to help children in step to see the good in their lives. We have to provide the structure within which the stepfamily can grow.

Chapter 11

STEP SIBLINGS: RIVALRY AND REVELRY

The relationship between step siblings can range from delight and love to jealousy, intrusion, hate, and even the desire for revenge. In many ways, the interaction of the step siblings becomes an intensified form of sibling rivalry. However, there is the added factor that someone else is sharing *my* father or *my* mother. Someone else is intruding upon *my* family. Someone else has moved into *my* home.

A lot changes when families combine. Both parents automatically acquire the added role of stepparent. As such they may be accused of cruelty to their partner's children and viewed as overindulgent to their own children. There doesn't have to be any evidence of this for the children to bring their charges. Instead, children often exhibit their own anxieties in their complaints.

Where Do I Belong?

The age lineup in a family is important in determining where a child fits in. Children become known as the oldest, the youngest, the middle child. They also become identified by their physical characteristics and their abilities.

Consider the family of single mother Dana. At thirteen, Jane may be the middle child, but she is the talented singer in the family. Terry, at nine, is the baby, and that is her niche. Jim is the oldest, sixteen, the only boy, and the big brother of the family.

In that family, the children all have their roles, from which they derive both a sense of security and the feeling of where they fit in. What happens when their mother marries Ed, who also has three children? If Ed has all girls, and if their ages range from ten to fifteen, then Dana's children will maintain their specific niches within the family. Jim will still be the only boy, the oldest and the big brother. Terry will remain the baby. Jane will be a middle child.

Of course, Ed's daughters will experience a reordering of *their* places. The oldest daughter will remain the oldest daughter, but she will no longer be the oldest *child*. Ed's youngest daughter will lose her place as the baby of the family. Aside from the normal problems of combining the lives of eight people (six children and two parents) into one unit, Ed's children will also have to cope with their loss of position.

Had Dana married someone with a son, Jim, although he might deny it, would have suffered a severe loss of status. He would no longer be the only boy. If the other boy were his age or older, the blow would have been compounded.

Further, if a child younger than Terry were to enter the home, her role as the baby would be eliminated. For years, she has gloried in the attention of the entire family, and she is still referred to as "the baby." If her mother had married someone who had a child younger than she, Terry would become a middle child.

The loss of status is considerable for all of these children. Even worse for a child to bear is the loss of the role of "only child."

The "Only Child" in Step

The only child has several levels of change with which to cope when his parent marries someone with children. First, as the only child, he has been the center of attention and the person who received all of the goodies. If he has lived in a single-parent household for several years, the child has also developed a strong role in the household decision making. He may have been asked to shoulder many of the household burdens, but the ego rewards have been an adequate compensation. Further, he has often acted more in the role of friend, even partner, than child. This description of the only child in the single-parent household applies to both boys and girls living with either male or female single parents.

The change to a multichild household is complicated by a severe decrease in his decision-making role. He also must give up many of his household tasks and, in the process, lose the attendant ego rewards. In addition, the only child may see his former role of friend and confidante usurped by the adult who is now the parent's partner.

In short, the only child is displaced. His old job description is invalid. He may feel he is invalid and/or replaced by the new partner.

Added to this displacement is the change in household composition that will require him to share his belongings, to share his home—perhaps his room—and to share his parent with others on a full-time basis.

Depending on the age of the only child, these changes can be heaven—or they can be hell.

On the other hand, growing up as an only child isn't always fun, and many such children yearn for brothers and sisters. They want someone to play with, to talk to, and fight with. With step siblings, the child doesn't have to start from scratch and wait until a baby grows old enough to join him. They may be right near your child's age, and the group may actually become instant companions.

And also, they may also become instant enemies. Step siblings are invaders in the territory of the only child. They will cramp his style, steal his space, and make him a less important and less doted-upon individual. Although you have to work to achieve harmony among the children, be aware of the great loss that the only child experiences when he enters a stepfamily. The only child is asked to accept situations that adults would rebel against in a business situation.

Sharing Your Space: Mary and Ginger

Consider Mary's position when her mother married John. Fifteen-year-old Mary and her mother lived in a two-bedroom apartment and managed their lives as a family for four years before Mary's mother and John married. For all of her fifteen years, Mary had occupied the same bedroom, decorating it as she wished and filling it with all of her treasures.

The marriage meant that John's twelve-year-old daughter, Ginger, would also be moving into their apartment. For Mary, that meant that her private space would have to be shared. She felt as if she were being attacked on all fronts. No longer would she and her mother share the intimacies of the past. No longer would she be making decisions as an adult. No longer was the apartment hers to walk around in as she pleased. Worst of all, she had no sanctuary to run to. There would always be Ginger.

Her mother took a direct stance when she told Mary about the proposed change:

"Mary, after John and I marry, you are going to be sharing your bedroom with Ginger. Now, I know that Ginger is younger than you are, and the bedroom has been yours for fifteen years. However, she *is* twelve, and that's not so young, and the two of you will just have to get along. I wish that we were financially able, but we can't afford to buy a new house. So, we'll all just work with what we *do* have."

Mary is not very happy about the change, and her mother's words are not going to make sharing her room any easier. The little talk, however, will help Mary to realize *why* she has to share her room. Her mother and John don't want to put her through an endurance test, nor is she being punished. Instead, there are circumstances that none of them can control at present.

But you must accept Mary's feelings of displacement and even anger. How would you feel if, after fifteen years of sitting at one desk in one office, you were told that someone else was now going to share your office and your desk? Not many of us could accept blithely. Still, we expect our children to accept blithely the changes that adding step siblings to the household require.

Rules for Step Siblings

There are three rules that seem to govern step sibling relationships:

1. Step siblings will get along very well because of or in spite of the parents.

2. Step sibling rivalry is only natural. This rivalry is due to the child's loss of position and his loss of the parent as the stepparent takes more of the parent's time. The intrusion of siblings who take time in the family, who take places at the table, who create a revolution in the rules of the house, and who turn the child's world upside down, make resentments, jealousies, and upsets surface in a very real way. The child is justified in his

feelings, and you can't deny him that. For the sake of the family, however, you must help him to accept the changes in the household, and it is your job to reorder the emotional atmosphere of the household.

3. Order in the household is vital. As parents, it is both your responsibility to decide the method of operation of the household. In many cases, guilt, lack of time, fear of alienating the child or hurting his self-esteem prevent parents from taking action. They fail to structure the household and neglect their responsibilities as heads of the household. The biological parent often feels such sympathy for his child that he fails to delineate the limits of behavior in the new household.

Before step sibling rivalry gets out of hand, even before you marry, you should set up the structure of the household. Pull out those job descriptions and decide what everyone is expected to do. Decide who will room with whom and how they are to manage their living accommodations. Review the ages of all of the children and publicly announce that a new order has emerged. The children already know this, but this public discussion will aid them in airing their concerns and fears. Set up rules of behavior that apply both to the parents and to the step siblings. Children should be told clearly that they are expected to speak respectfully. Manners must always be minded and rights respected.

The adults make the rules. Once guidelines are in place, a more materially and psychologically ordered existence will follow.

A natural rivalry exists between step siblings, just as there is a rivalry between natural siblings. However, the step rivalry may often seem worse.

Sex and Step Siblings

Step siblings are not blood relations. They have sometimes not even been brought up near each other. So, what's wrong if they feel sexually attracted to each other and they act on that attraction? A lot is wrong, and a lot more can go wrong.

Incest taboos have predominated in society for a good reason. Not only does the taboo protect the weaker members of the family from being exploited, but the existence of an incest taboo helps people to live together in intimacy without concern about sexual interaction.

It is understandably difficult for young people who are not related to be thrown together in the intimate situation of sharing a home. They are conveniently available to one another, yet they are functioning in the roles of siblings. Acting on their attraction can spell trouble.

Keep in mind that spontaneous sexual intimacy between step siblings can leave one partner badly hurt by the experience. It may be experimentation, but there is a strong chance that one step sibling will want to continue the relationship while the other will want to end it. How do you break up with a stepsister or stepbrother? The results of this can create a battleground in the home that can doom the step relationship.

You have to extend the incest taboo to the stepfamily and set rules that will aid step siblings in avoiding the problems. Try the following guidelines:

1. No one should be permitted to run around in underwear.
2. After a certain hour, everyone must stay in his/her own bedroom.
3. Children of the same sex will share each bedroom.
4. No sibling can just walk into another sibling's bedroom without knocking.

As stepparents, you must accept that some "givens" come with the stepfamily relationship. Sibling rivalry is natural among biological siblings. With the heightened emotional atmosphere of step, it should be expected that the problem would extend to the step siblings and be even worse.

You should also expect that sexual attraction will emerge between adolescent and teenage step siblings who are forced into an intimacy with what may amount to total strangers. You have to expect this, but it is your role to take the necessary steps to prevent them from acting upon their attraction.

The household must have a plan of operation that provides direction for both roles and responsibilities, and this need extends to the step sibling situation. With the proper guidance and emotional support, both step sibling rivalry and revelry can be avoided.

Fighting Between Kids

It has become almost fashionable—we'd say neglectful—to allow children to fight, talk rudely to each other, argue loudly, and even seriously hit each other.

Parents, in your house, this is not allowed. If kids are going to fight, let them do so when you do not see it. If you see it, you stop it. You punish them. Don't expect to mete out justice.

Chapter 12

HANDLING THE PRIOR SPOUSE

There are no ex-parents, only ex-spouses. However, for as long as your children are minors, your ex-spouse and your partner's can be important influences on your present relationship. If the relationship ended because of divorce, you continue to be mother, father, and child, even long after you have ceased to be husband and wife. Both exes, both parents, in the best interests of the child, must put aside old anger and co-parent. That is if you want children who feel good about themselves and have high self-esteem.

The situation is different in many of its aspects when the prior spouse has died.

Exorcising Ghosts

The prior spouse who has died is not a constant and living presence who sends you snide remarks via the children, nor is he/she there to point out your failures in raising the children. The prior spouse who has died is physically absent, but that could make him/her even more potent a presence.

When the prior spouse has died, many myths arise to surround the children's memory of that person. In some cases, you may also begin to believe the myths about your former spouse, making the going very rough for your current partner. This is a mistake, and one that only you can correct.

Children, especially stepchildren, tend to idealize every memory of their late parents. He was tall, handsome, noble, brave, intelligent, and generous. She was svelte, beautiful, noble, brave, intelligent, and generous. The people remembered by the stepchild are of heroic proportions. One stepchild talked frequently of her late mother, someone she remembered as a beautiful woman who was charming at parties and loved by everyone she met. She was gracious, adored, and kind, and the child said that she missed her terribly. When someone asked her how old she had been when her mother died, she turned to the questioner and answered, "Six months old."

She was too young to remember anything about her mother. Yet, she had pieced together a goddess from the remembrances of others and out of the deep well of her own need.

As the stepparent to such a child, there is no reality that you can offer that will effectively combat the myth. It is cruel even to try. Let the child sustain the myth and even allow it to grow. This is necessary to the child's self-esteem. Whatever the late biological parent may have been, marvelous or terrible, the stepparent has to accept the child's myth and the fact that it is fueled by a great love for the dead parent. Respect the child's feelings. Reassure him that you understand his feelings for the parent. You are not going to try to replace that parent. No one really could.

Show him that you don't want to push the memory of the late parent out his mind. Ask for a favorite picture of the parent and go with the child to select a beautiful frame to fit that picture.

Select what pleases him. Then join with the child in finding a place in his/her room for the framed picture.

Another sticky area is when you marry into a family in which the prior spouse has died in the home. Ideally, the new family should have a new home. Economically, it is not always feasible. So, if you do move into the home that the prior spouse decorated, maintained and lived in, go slowly in attempting to make it your own.

Children become attached to the way a home looks, feels, and smells. Moving in and redecorating immediately may be taken as a great insult to their late parent. It may even shake up your new spouse.

Instead of walking in with *your* ideas, solicit *their* ideas. Changes will have to be made, but delicacy and the desire for peace in the family require that you move softly and cautiously. Align the family with you and get the children in on the redecorating. When they have made it *their* home, and when the changes are gradual, children can more easily accept them.

The Divorced Prior Spouse

Divorce is totally different. In divorce, the prior spouse is alive and very often lives nearby. The children see him or her periodically and there exists the whole problem of visitation. You can't just put a picture in the child's room, speak respectfully of the prior spouse, and hope to make the situation work. Instead, you are faced with children who shuttle between households, alimony, and child support payments, what to do about holidays, and the realm of difficulties that have been catalogued throughout this book.

One important caution for the stepparent, and even for the biological parent, is that "bad-mouthing" the prior spouse to the children is unwise. The children already have been traumatized by the divorce and the remarriage, they already know that not all of the adults involved were angels, and they already know that not everybody loves everybody else. Why force them into the position of having to defend the prior spouse while you attack him/her?

The major issue between prior spouses is often money. When a man remarries and comes to the new relationship with alimony and child support obligations, he comes with limited resources. No matter how successful he has become, he may well be starting out with less available money than in the first marriage. This is sure to affect his feelings about having more children, spending habits, and other financial matters. Many second wives have found that they have to work to keep their marriages going financially. With all of his prior obligations, there's little money left over for the new marriage. That thought creates a lot of hostility in women. It also undermines the man's role in the family.

The second wife is not the only one who may be bitter. The first wife often comes out of the older marital system in which the wife did not work, and she thus may have no marketable skills. She may not have the training needed to find a good job, and she may be going through the whole displaced-homemaker syndrome. There is also the problem that the court systems do not always award people the amount of money needed to support a family. So, the first wife may also be a bitter lady.

You've also got a bitter man, because none of us can keep up with what life costs. He may rationally acknowledge that his former wife hasn't been in the workplace for fifteen years and has to be trained for a job. He may also acknowledge that, at best, she will make $175 to $200 weekly as a secretary and that this amount isn't going to go too far. However, making payments to her and keeping up his present household puts severe strain on him.

Everybody has a cause for complaint, and everybody often does complain. However, instead of blaming the cause for all of this ugliness, the economics of divorce, we often take to blaming each other. The children, who already may be suffering self-esteem problems, listen to us degrade a prior spouse in one household, then visit the other household on weekends and hear the same complaints in reverse.

That is not fair to the children. They didn't create the situation, but they may suffer the most.

If you are the new spouse, either stepmother or stepfather, you should keep in mind that these two people had an important relationship for several years. They created children together, and they have a bond that is very difficult to break. There are many suppressed regrets and feelings of guilt that continue to surround the breakup.

Many new wives and stepmothers complain that their husband turns into a wimp when the former wife calls. He says "yes" to everything and gives in to her. After he hangs up, he is a diminished man in his new wife's eyes.

New wives become infuriated with the former spouse for turning their husband into something they don't want to see. This strong, wonderful man is suddenly perceived as weak.

Many new husbands and stepfathers complain that their wives let the former husband get away with murder over child support payments and other obligations. They feel insecure about the depth of the former relationship and may accuse the prior spouse of poisoning the minds of the stepchildren against them.

No one can determine who is right in these situations and who is wrong. Perhaps we should not even try. To try to sort out the wrongs may only provide a temporary bandage to a serious cut.

Complaining does no good. Bad-mouthing the prior spouse does no good. Burdening the children with messages does no good.

The Obligation to Parent with Your Ex

The adults have to come to the understanding that it is the well-being of the children that should be uppermost in their minds. From that premise, they should establish firmly the rights and responsibilities of all parents and stepparents in the situation. Everyone has certain roles and obligations and they should agree to fulfill those responsibilities. When they don't, appropriate consequences should follow. This is another area in which it is up to the adults to set the boundaries and to do the work needed to make the situation as peaceful as possible for the children.

Chapter 13

RITUALS IN STEP

Rituals are comforting to many of us because they give our lives a feeling of continuity that may often be obscured in the step situation. Holiday dinners, birthday parties, social functions, even daily rituals such as family meals occur with regularity and give us security. In the step situation, while such rituals may continue, they are often weighed down with the confusion of family relationships and feelings.

Holidays and Traditional Family Celebrations

Holidays and traditional family times are difficult in the step-family because they are by nature family-centered. In the step situation, what constitutes family can have a wide range of meanings.

How do we celebrate rituals and share our special days with "family" without hurting each other and the people we love? This is a tough question to answer. These events often seem to invite and to exacerbate discord and disappointment in the stepfamily, rather than bring joy, because they only emphasize that the family is no longer the same.

No matter how we look forward to the day, and no matter how well-meaning our intentions, the mood is often disturbing. There are enough horrendous modern-day Christmas stories to challenge the grimness of both Scrooge and the Grinch.

Instead of sugar plums dancing in their heads, children in step situations may more often be kept awake through the anxiety of wondering how their day will go. Because of their often divided loyalties, and the shuttling back and forth between parents, children in step situations usually dread the day, and their behavior shows this. Their chameleonlike emotions make their parents wary of holidays.

Christmas, Chanukah, Easter, Passover, and other formal holidays are not the only days of dread. Birthdays take on a new meaning in step.

The child's birthday should be a day of celebration and love. For many children, it is often a day in which they must choose between a birthday party thrown by Mommy or by Daddy, and time spent with *either* but not with *both*. Both parents and their new partners may sincerely want to help the child celebrate his birthday, but without cooperation and concern for the child, they will only succeed in making him feel anxious, guilty, and deeply angry that his day can't be simpler.

Not everybody can host the birthday party, but the parents can arrange to celebrate the ritual in a variety of ways. The parents can agree to celebrate the child's birthday as part of one big group in which the fighting is temporarily forgotten in the festivity. Another option is for each to host a small and separate party to which different people have been invited, with adequate consideration for the stamina of the child.

Other options also exist, but they require that the *adults,* biological parents and stepparents, negotiate the situation. The child should not be placed in the no-win situation of having to choose between Mommy's party and Daddy's party. Given that choice, the child would rather stay in his room and forget all about his birthday.

A similar no-win situation is frequently created for the child on other holidays. Is it Christmas with Daddy because two holidays are guaranteed in the settlement? Or is it Christmas with Mommy, because Daddy had another important holiday? Who chooses? The child may often be given that thankless role.

Instead of blocking off the holidays and forcing the child to spend Christmas at only one location, negotiation is again in order. Keep in mind that the welfare of your child, and not the selfish aims of the parents or stepparents, should be most important in deciding what to do about holidays and other traditional family celebrations.

Give the child as much of *everybody* as you can, within reason and after careful consideration of the child's age and ability to handle all the excitement. One way of compromising would be to spend half of the day here and the other half there. Perhaps, however great the sacrifice, the child should be allowed to enjoy the actual holiday in his full-time home, but spend the evening or the day after with the rest of the family.

When you create the arrangements that holidays and traditional celebrations require, consider the arrangements from the perspective of the child. Put your own concerns aside for a time.

Day by Day

Although we rarely view the acts of daily life as ritual, much of what we do comprises a pattern that gives our lives a continuity that all of us need. We worship God in a specific place at specific times of the week, month, or year. We plant flowers in specific seasons. We visit family and friends according to specific, if emotional, timetables. And so on.

The Meal

One important ritual in the home, and one that has been largely lost in the hustle of everyday life, is that of the family meal. Everybody runs out of the house at different times in the morning, so breakfasts are rarely eaten together. Work and school keep us away from the home, so lunch is alone. Dinner is rarely convenient for all members of the family at any one time, so everybody eats at a different hour and even at a different place.

In this nation, it is only at some dinners and perhaps at a Saturday or Sunday brunch that we can expect that the whole family (or, at least, most of it) will be gathered around the table for a meal. It is essential that family members come together regularly to maintain and to build upon that sense of family. The best place to do this is while enjoying the ritual of a meal. For the stepfamily, it's vital.

The ritual of meals brings the family closer together. If your mealtimes are unpleasant, it's time to make some changes.

Not all meals can be eaten together, but special care should be taken for those that are shared. For special times, the table should be attractively set with a pretty cloth, the silver, nice dinnerware, and candles. For a less formal meal, some of this can be omitted, but the feeling of ritual should be maintained in some way. Everyone in the family should have some part in preparing for the meal.

The cook should be aided by helpers who will chop food, fetch items, set the table, and shop for the meal. There can be a salad maker or other helper. Divide the preparation of the meal up into seven parts and see how you can involve all family members in the process. Assign duties as they seem appropriate to the skills and interests of different family members.

Sharing the ritual of meals should mean that everyone views the time as something to which they look forward. A certain code of dress and cleanliness is necessary, and all family members should know this in advance. "No torn jeans and sweaty sweatshirts at the table." "Clean hands and wrists." "No 'boom boxes' or other electronic equipment." "Even if the '49ers *are* playing, you can't bring the portable TV into the room. Next time tell us in advance, and we'll all try to accommodate you by changing the time." And so on.

A ritual also requires that certain rules of behavior exist. Family members shouldn't feel that they can straggle in whenever they choose, but they should know that they will be given a five-minute warning before the meal will be put on the table. In that five minutes, they should wrap up whatever they are doing and prepare for the meal.

Order is very important to mealtime because meals in a stepfamily can often turn to brawls. You and your partner should structure these meals and plan what will go on at the table. Of first importance is establishing who sits where. Switching seats may provide variety, but it also causes arguments when a favorite seat is taken. Everyone should have a specific seat and must sit in it. This eliminates bad surprises such as having a table full of howling children who are all accusing each other of seat stealing: "Johnny's in my seat!" "Well, Mary's in my seat!" "How come he always gets the seat he wants?" Is this scene familiar?

The meal is not only a time to eat but should give stepfamily members an opportunity to sit together and to talk. A lot of things can be discussed at the table. You can share the details of your day, and tell other family members of both the good and the bad things that happened. You may ask or give advice. The conversation may be heavy or light.

Whichever direction the mealtime discussion takes, certain rules have to exist to guide it. All family members should be expected to treat each other with respect and to view sharing the meal as an enjoyable experience in which they savor both the meal and each other's company.

We can share both bad and good news, but some restrictions should exist. Mealtime is not the time for a gripe session or for verbal or other abuse. Children should know that some things are considered inappropriate at the table.

You do not discuss anything that will disrupt the digestive process. Save the disgusting for later.

You do not say, "Sam, you're a jerk," or "I can't stand you, stepmother/stepfather/whomever."

You do not dominate the conversation, but you share with everyone else, so that everyone participates.

As parents, you and your partner have to set the rules and see that the children comply. As the male and female heads of the household, you should sit at opposite ends of the table and keep your eyes on all of the children, or on one of them or on the little one, or whatever arrangement you feel is necessary to give needed structure to the meal.

In some ways, the structure of the table at mealtimes is a good example of the structure of the family at other times. The mealtime order reflects the emotional, psychological, and physical ordering of the stepfamily. Pay attention to it.

Remember, once the rules are set, children who break the rules should be asked to leave the table. You may not want that to happen, but once children are told the consequences of inappropriate behavior at the table you have to follow through.

Similarly, once we sit down at the table, we should ask to be excused if we want to leave the table. It is not only a matter of manners, but adherence to certain rules of behavior increases the feeling of mealtimes together as a ritual. This is important. Mealtimes are the only time in everyone's busy schedule when the stepfamily, and all families, can really work on those very tender and tenuous personal relationships of the family.

The Rituals of Visitation

Rituals of visitation? Yes, and in the best sense of the word *ritual*. A ritual provides a sense of security and continuity by its very nature of being an expected happening. In ritual, certain specified actions are required of you, and you come to know when, where, and how everything will happen.

If that doesn't sound like your experiences with visitation, don't worry. Most visitation experiences are loosely planned and really give the child and the parents very little to anticipate. Such looseness, however, leaves too much to chance and agitates everyone involved.

It is difficult for a child to shift gears from his five-day-a-week home to the visitation home. Rhythms are different. Procedures change. How can anyone be expected to become one of the family when there are no guides to tell him what being one of this visitation family means? To provide the niche for the visitation child, and to make visitation an enjoyable and caring experience, you must develop *rituals* to which all of you can look forward and toward for structure.

Just as we know when holidays and birthdays are coming, children should know when visitation will occur and be encouraged to plan for it. Each visitation experience should follow roughly the same routine so that the child knows what to expect. Surprises, when added to the shifts that must occur in the life of the visiting child, are not always welcome.

Let the child know where he fits in from the start. He should have certain duties to perform when he is visiting, not so much because you need the help, but more because these are his way of joining the circle of the household.

If the visits are only for a day, you should plan to have one special *ritual* meal each time. During this time, you review the week, share feelings, and discuss life in general. This should be *alone time* with the biological parent. Later in the day, time with the stepparent can be led into, and the group can take part in a pre-planned activity.

It may be possible, and it is desirable, that everyone then share a meal or snack before the visiting child leaves. It is a way to "debrief"—go over what happened and what will happen next time. In this way, another part of the ritual is born, and there is another certainty to which the child—and the stepfamily—can look forward.

When the visitation is for a weekend, more planning is needed, but there is also more time for ritual—and relationship-building. Certain actions should occur every time the child arrives for visitation. He should hang his coat in his specific place and take his possessions to his specific room. Then, the visitation should be initiated with some sort of ritual, even if it is only milk and cookies in the kitchen. In time, this will become a happily anticipated beginning to visitation. It is also a time to go over visitation plans.

As far as possible, visitation weekends should follow a consistent pattern. You may choose to eat in on Friday night, sleep late on Saturday, have a family brunch midday on Saturday or Sunday, take walks, have dinner out, and many other activities. These are the areas in which rituals should be developed.

Create a pattern that both you and the visiting child can follow, and punctuate that pattern with special times of closeness. Every Saturday (or, Sunday, if you like) should contain a specially prepared, lazy brunch, during which you share good food and good feelings.

Every Saturday or Sunday should contain one or more special times of sharing. This does not have to mean a trip to the circus, a zoo, a play, a movie, or Disneyland. It may be any one of these each weekend, but it can also be the weekly chess game, the weekly walk and splurge at an ice cream shop, the weekly visit to a friend or relative. Where you go and what you do is not so important as the fact that this is something that you do together. It is a ritual.

The planning of visitation doesn't have to be rigid. It also shouldn't be as loose as many people allow it to be. Most parents involved in visitation claim that they want to just be "natural" with their children; then they let guilt overtake them and they become Disneyland Daddies and Mommies. Some of this is appropriate; most is not.

Planning and allowing the child to know what is expected of him is enormously important to a pleasant visitation experience.

Although much of the focus on visitation ritual has been on the noncustodial parent, the custodial parent should also create rituals around it. Before your child leaves for visitation, you and your partner should have a ritual meal with him. The family should gather around and give the child a secure feeling that he is leaving this home for a time, but that loving and caring people will be here when he returns. The situation isn't easy. However, angrily hustling a child out of the house to the waiting parent makes it even harder for the child caught in the middle.

When the visiting child returns, he is often very upset. He has to shift gears again. He may fear being pumped for information. He may feel guilty and disloyal if he had a good time. Don't add to his anxiety. Instead, make a ritual of his homecoming by having a regularly planned meal or snack at which he can unwind and begin to ease back into your home.

Rituals. They are not just for birthdays and regularly scheduled holidays. They help us to live our lives with some sort of certainty. Because the stepfamily has little shared history of its own, the rituals that it shares at the outset can only be general. These are part of what everyone else experiences. Instead, we need to create rituals that are ours alone, to draw each other closer together, and to move us even closer to being a unit with its own history. We need to become a family—one that happens to be made up of people who are living in step.

Chapter 14

STEP ETIQUETTE

"I wanna sit next to Daddy!"

"I don't want *him* here!"

"Who invited *her?*"

"Why isn't Daddy here yet?"

"My teacher wants to see my *mother*—you're not my mother!"

For many couples who are either dating or married, these constitute the sounds of step. Children demand to sit where they want to, forcing the stepparent out whenever possible. They protest having a parent's partner present. Sometimes they spend endless hours waiting for a visitation parent who doesn't show up or who fails even to call. They also must deal with the sticky situation of who should sign the report card, who goes to parent-teacher conferences, and who gets the progress reports.

The Need for an Etiquette of Step

Children become upset about these situations, and they should. When there is no mechanism set up to handle a situation, a free-for-all results. Solving the problems and eliminating these concerns takes a certain kind of structuring, a code of behavior called *step etiquette*.

Most of us try to function according to the patterns of behavior that we learned as children. As society changes, so does what is permitted in society. Etiquette changes, too. What was permissible in the intact biological family becomes intolerable in the step situation.

Consider this example. Five-year-old Jimmy is in his "I-love-Mommy/you-go-away-Daddy" stage and squeezes between his parents as they hug and kiss each other in greeting. His little body pushes them apart. His parents look down at him, embrace him, and pull him toward them both.

Replay that scene in a step situation. Jimmy is still five years old and in the same stage. He squeezes between his mother and her partner as they hug and kiss each other in greeting. The two adults look down at him, feeling intruded upon. His mother feels guilty and her partner feels insulted.

Jimmy doesn't know that he shouldn't push his mother and her partner apart, because no one has ever told him so. The natural parents don't feel the same sensitivity that a stepparent may feel, and his mother may also be overly sensitive about Jimmy's actions. Poor little Jimmy then finds that, while his action in the first version is "cute," it is "naughty" in the second.

Similarly, thoughtlessness may be more easily forgiven in the intact family than it will be in the stepfamily or in visitation situations. If Daddy or Mommy forgets to tell the child about a change of plans in the intact family, there is always tomorrow to make it up. When visitation hurts and omissions occur, making the pain go away takes a greater and different kind of effort.

The step situation changes the rules of behavior in many other ways. The old rules don't apply, and trying to use them to deal with the new issues of step often leaves you helpless. Instead, you should be writing up a new etiquette for your new situation, a step etiquette.

10 Classic "Bad" Manners of the Divorced and Stepfamily

The children of divorce are damaged not only by the loss of self-esteem that goes on before and after the divorce, but also what happens following the breakup. Here are a list of the "classic" bad manners, bad habits, bad rituals, or no rituals.

1. *Few or no meals, together.* Traditionally the family meal was the place of intimacy, the time when we brought our victories and wounds to the family for applause and advice. It was a time of sharing, of learning the values that only a family can teach a child. These "family values" were most often heard, talked about, and discussed at the meal.

2. *Family values, mores, and ways of thinking have become TV dominated.* Today we see kid and grownups coming home at odd hours, grabbing food catch as catch can, and racing to their separate rooms and TV shows.

3. *Discipline or guidance is severely lacking.* In the old days, when homemaking was considered a valued and significant position, Mother and Father gave the child things to do, contributions to make, chores to complete, and rules to abide by. Manners and respect were expected and taught.

Does anyone remember that "look" from Dad when you did something wrong or said something "smart" to Mom or a sibling? This discipline socialized us for the greater world: the world of school, sports, and, later, business. Today we see too many couch-potato kids who will not even participate in sports. Rationalization, blaming, and excuses are typical. As the family all too rarely instills these values we find many young people unable to function well in the workplace. When the number reaches a "critical mass" the society's ability to produce goods and services will diminish. Many say we see this already today.

4. *The child becomes the center of attention, not the parent or couple.* This is a classic syndrome of the divorce epidemic. Each parent fears the loss of the child. Everyone feels guilty. As a result, the child becomes the center of the family universe, hogging attention at the dinner table and elsewhere, interrupting unabashedly.

5. *Couples fail to restructure their new families.* In the merger of his and her way, we tend to make our way "right." Indeed, to make the stepfamily work we must honor each way and, like a Chinese menu, take and agree upon a little from column A *and* column B—the man's way and the woman's way.

6. *Lack of civility and the resultant lack of co-parenting between ex spouses* damages their children. In this society dominated by "yellow, sensationalist" media, we have come to believe that it is our "right" and perfectly normal to hate, or "bad-mouth," or put down, our ex-spouse, the parent of our children. Often the ex deserves the putdowns for what s/he may or may not have done. However, not in front, or within earshot of, the children. These bad manners damage that which we say we love the most: our children.

7. *Visitation schedules are not upheld.* All too many ex-spouses and guilty dads try to "move around" visitation schedules. Of course, sometimes this is necessary, but it must not be the norm. We say that visitation schedules need to be cast in cement. For example, pick up at six P.M. on Friday night and delivery at six P.M. on Sunday night. Who picks up, who

delivers must be defined in the agreement. No loose ends! The lack of predictability is one of the greatest enemies to the child's self-esteem.

8. *The inability to have a conversation.* Parents are so other directed that few teach children the art and politeness of conversation. They use "you" messages, blaming, shaming, and demeaning when we do not agree, as opposed to the polite forms of conversation, which begin with not, "You are wrong . . . " but with "I believe," "I think" or "I feel." Therein we take responsibility for our point of view but allow others their points of view. This is an interchange, rather than a confrontation.

9. *The accepted desire not to be part of the family and withdraw.* Parents should not allow children to run to their rooms and withdraw from the world of social interchange to isolation. We are seeing a generation of people who have few social skills, have never experienced good conversations, and use that as an excuse to continue the behavior rather than to learn new ways of interacting. Many have never purchased or even opened a book on etiquette.

10. *What happened to a sense of humor* without putdowns, or a belief in a Higher Power that allows us to accept rather than to retaliate? The responsibility for the outcomes we achieve is ours and ours alone.

The Etiquette of Dating—and Sex

Children should not be involved in the dating relationships, but they should be included. They need to be around the person whom their parent is dating, even if the relationship is only casual, because they are an important part of your life. To keep everyone comfortable, however, a little preparation is necessary.

Your child should be present when your date arrives and they should interact for fifteen minutes or more. Encourage your child to welcome the date with a "hello" and a handshake. If you are not ready, and if your child is old enough, he may assume the role of host and offer to take your date's coat and to get something to drink. As a parent, you should be glad to give your child the opportunity of learning how to conduct pleasant and polite conversation, and of learning how to make guests welcome.

Presenting a date to your child for the first time can be a little tricky. Everyone may know about everyone else, but the formal presentation can be tense. It can be planned or spur-of-the-moment. However the first encounter comes about, take the opportunity to say simply, as Emily Post recommends, " 'This is Maurice Williams, a friend of Mommy's,' " or " 'Daddy's friend, Margery Glass, has wanted to meet you.' "

Once you are dating for a while, your child will fall into his own patterns of interacting with your date. Whatever evolves, it is your role to see that such interaction is respectful and polite.

The real test of the dating relationship comes when you have your first "date" as a threesome. That's when problems of conflicting loyalties and the need to share attention emerge. The child wants his parent's attention, but he may also be intrigued by the new adult. However intriguing, though, that new adult does constitute a rival for his parent, so the child is not going to stray too far from Mommy or Daddy.

Who gets to sit next to you in the car? How do you arrange seating at the movies? Whom do you answer first?

Everybody wants to come first, but only one person can. Who will that person be? If you give your attention to your child, your date will feel excluded. If your attention goes to the date, your child will feel excluded. Both will probably act out, and you will feel like deserting them both on the spot.

As the link between the two, you have to communicate to both your child and your date that you will be playing two roles simultaneously. That's not an easy trick. Yet, the alternative is disaster.

Remember that your child is confused by your changing roles

and his responses are often just as confused. He may want a new adult in his life, but he doesn't want to share you with that new adult nor does he particularly like the closeness and urgency that he may sense. His mind starts to work overtime with questions of where he fits in, why you aren't always acting like "Mommy" or "Daddy" all the time, or if he will lose you.

When children sense that the new relationship may be serious, their responses become very defensive. They may be extremely rude. They may sulk, cry, have nightmares, fear going to sleep or refuse to eat. They will throw tantrums in your date's presence. When that happens, calmly deal with the situation at the moment. Lovingly take your child aside and take a moment to explain. Assure him of your love. Proceed slowly.

What happens when a relationship begins to mean sleepovers, and the sleepovers are at your home? How you handle it depends on the age of your children. Children of all ages can sense the feelings that occur between their parent and another adult, but there is no reason to inform your child of an ongoing sexual relationship. Keep the night noises down to a minimum. The best way to handle this is to be discreet and concentrate on the friendship angle.

One parent handled the situation in a slightly devious but admirable way:

"I remember when I was single and my child was still quite young. I would often do things that were not quite 'honest.' Nonetheless, I felt they were in the best interests of my son.

"When the man in my life would spend the night, I would ask him to dress while I went into my son's bedroom and closed the door for a little good morning chat. I would glibly inform him that John was on his way over for breakfast, and I would suggest that we get the table set.

"In the meanwhile, my friend would find his way to the local bakery and then reappear laden with delicious goodies for the three of us. In this way, *my* friend became and stayed *our* friend.

More important, my son was not confused and excluded from a relationship that he could not possibly understand."

Older children can't be so easily fooled, but then they can be talked to in a different manner. Your child should not be made to feel put out, nor should he be forced to come to terms with explicit sexuality. Discretion is the key. When carefully planned, such situations can make everyone happy.

What's in a Name?

What everyone in the stepfamily calls each other should be discussed before setting up housekeeping. Nothing can stir the blood in anger more easily than an angry child complaining to his father or mother about what *"he"* or *"she"* did in tones that drip with contempt. A name should be determined at the outset, whether it be the stepparent's first name, a term that signifies closeness, or a nickname. Whatever is decided upon should be used with respect in the home, and it may change as the relationship of the stepfamily changes.

It is important in step that we know how to introduce each other. For a long time the very use of the word step has been avoided. This avoidance of who we are in the family situation may often lead to confusion and upset. Since there are such a large number of individuals who live in step, it is now important to address the issue and use the word.

In most of the cultures in the world the step situation is seen in a negative light. The French, however, have a wonderful way of thinking about step. In French steps are called *belle mère* and *beau père, belle fille,* and *beau fils,* which translated mean beautiful mother and beautiful father, beautiful daughter and beautiful son. In English step doesn't mean beautiful, but we can uplift the word by using a positive voice tone when we introduce each other.

Step people may introduce each other in two different ways:

Mrs. Jones says, "This is my stepdaughter, Wendy." Or she may say, "This is my husband John's daughter, Wendy." It is not recommended that children introduce stepparents by their first names—but the adults must decide, taking into consideration the feelings of the child, how the child should introduce them. Again we encourage the use of step in an "up" tone: "This is my stepdad, Timothy Hanson."

We cannot stress enough that introductions and titles are important. Adults must decide. Children must be taught and not left up to their own devices.

The way we introduce each other in public indicates how we feel about each other. Therefore, grownups must watch their voice tone and children must be caringly instructed.

In my own case, the choice of names for my stepfather came about gradually. My mother once came to me and said my stepfather, whom I called Russell, would just love my calling him Dad. I thought about that for a long period of time, then decided, "Oh, well, I'll call my father Daddy, and I can call him Dad." One day, after quite a bit of thinking—I was well into my twenties at the time—I turned to him and said something like, "Dad, can you help me with the car?" He just beamed.

For your family, using "Dad" and "Mom" for the stepparents might not be comfortable. First names are fine. Or create a term with which everyone agrees—said with respect.

All-Occasion Etiquette

Joyous occasions take on new meaning when stepfamilies are involved. Graduation ceremonies and parties, school plays and weddings should be times of celebration that are planned well in advance. Because of the problems that "Whom do we invite?" causes, however, many people put off their planning until the last minute. They somehow feel that the hostilities, hurt feelings, and other emotional outgrowths of the step situation will go away if they are ignored.

The first difficult occasion is usually the step wedding. Do the children attend? Which relatives do you invite? Who is still talking to whom?

The Wedding

The etiquette of remarriage has changed drastically since the 1960s. Today remarrying couples may plan any kind of wedding they want. It is our recommendation that it be a celebration that includes the children. Often in the past, couples married and told the children . . . after. Not appropriate. Children, if you want them to start out supporting the marriage, need to be made part of the joyous event.

Little ones, even if the wedding is small, should be made flower girls and ring bearers. Older children are asked to attend and participate.

If the groom is divorced and the bride is marrying for the first time, she should feel no restrictions as to the degree of festivity.

In the past, if the bride was divorced and had children, the wedding was kept small and informal. This is no longer a hard and fast rule.

Telling the Children

The children are to be the first to know of the wedding. Often they are frightened. They fear a loss of their place in their parent's heart. In addition, most children still wish for Mommy and Daddy to get back together. Marriage now squashes the child's hopes, and this may devastate him. In addition to the emotional disruptions are the physical disruptions: moves, new people in his/her house, another child in a room that was just his/hers, and the loss of his/her position in the family. The oldest child may become the second oldest, and the baby may lose his/her position as the youngest.

If all that isn't enough, there may be a strange adult—someone who you're not sure you can trust and who doesn't love you—and who is not your mother or your father—telling you what to do. The result could be the beginning of bad feelings about step and the stepperson.

It is important to listen to the child's feeling and fears and then to go on and reassure him/her that we will and can work it out. All too often children's fears of the loss of us, territory, turf, and inheritance stops the parent from remarrying. It should not be the child who decides on the remarriage, but the parent.

It is normal for the child to be concerned and unhappy. It is then important to describe what life will be like for the child in the new circumstances and assure him that all *will* be well. We must say this even if we know that children often know better . . . and if we ourselves are concerned about step. The child needs to be told something like the old saying: "All beginnings are difficult" . . . but we will be just fine. As adults we know we need not share our concerns about remarriage with the child. We should only give children the problems they can do something about. Our heavier concerns or problems we can share with another adult or a step counselor.

Including the Children in the Ceremony

Next it is important to include even the reluctant child in on some of the plans for the festivities, no matter how small the wedding. Once made part of, as opposed to feeling left out of the plans, the child often will begin to enjoy the ritual.

Children should be included and encouraged to participate in the wedding, as long as they want to—as flower girl and ring bearer if they are young, and as junior bridesmaid and usher if they are older. Approval from the other parent should be obtained before asking the child to participate. Otherwise the child will be conflicted in his/her loyalties by having that choice.

Even if they do not serve as attendants, the children should attend the parent's wedding. This enables them to adjust to the new stepfamily situation more easily.

The Honeymoon

Many couples delay their honeymoon, or keep it short, until the children have begun to become more adjusted to the new stepfamily. We recommend this especially when young children are involved. It's a major change, and a honeymoon and the parent's leaving them is just too much, too soon.

Of course, if the couple has been living together for quite some time, and the children are adjusted to the new step situation, the rules change.

Good references for all of the details of a remarriage are Emily Post's or Amy Vanderbilt's books on etiquette.

Pre-Planned Solution

The first dinner with the children is planned. Father and stepmother know of some of the potential pitfalls. They have gotten counseling prior to the remarriage and learned about the possible unpredictable responses of the girls to their Dad's new marriage; their feelings of loss, fears of losing Daddy, etc. . . . Dad has talked to them alone and has allowed and encouraged them to come forth with their concerns. He has assured them of his love and asked them to be mannerly with his new wife, whether they feel good about it or not. Dad reminds himself about seeing what is going on. He does not expect Sandy to behave like their mother only better. All of them have learned how step functions differently from their prior family. Daddy has his girls and Sandy "psyched" to make this first dinner together a good one.

Sandy and Bob are careful to allow time after the girls leave to carefully go over from each person's point of view what went wrong and what went right. They then plan the next visit. This all takes vision, planning, and time.

After-the-Fact Solution

The situation has occurred. Past tense. Somewhere along the way they realize this is not working the way they expected it to. It is not working like an intact family. This is a classic step situation where Bob's reality is one thing and Sandy's is another. It is not inconsequential that the children's reality is totally different.

Sandy and Bob need to sit down and calmly see and hear each other's realities from each other's point of view. This is done without interruption and without redefining the realities and without injections. Here they begin to notice the acute differences in their points of view.

They try to keep the atmosphere of the discussion respectful— they know that their expectations are out of line with the reality of step, and they are disappointed when they expect each other to behave like the typical family. Now they go into carefully creating their vision for the next weekend—planning activities—who will do what. They build mutual couple strength by deciding what will be appropriate manners, behavior, and responsibilities in this house. They also plan a system of signaling each other when any behavior becomes cause for concern. Then they agree to excuse themselves, should this behavior occur, and decide immediately what their actions will be to redirect the behavior into their original game plan. Should discipline be necessary in the step family, the couple decides and agrees what is appropriate behavior, and the biological parent, not the stepparent, metes out the discipline.

Visitation Etiquette

Just as there should be rituals in visitation, there is also a need for a special etiquette for visitation. Good visitation doesn't just happen without planning.

Do you pick up the child? Or does he just "arrive"? Should your partner be present? Or does visitation just belong to the biological parent and not to the step? What happens when visitation is disrupted?

These are only a few of the questions that parents and stepparents ask about the visitation process. It is an emotional issue, for parents and children and for the stepfamily.

It is strange that we may sympathize with the corporate executive who must travel, but we expect children to adapt readily to moving from one house to another in visitation. Not only are they physically inconvenienced, but they have to confront their changed family every time they enter Mommy or Daddy's new home and see Mommy or Daddy's new family. The child has to endure both the difficulties of visitation and contend with the step situation. Do you wonder why they act out?

Everyone has rights in the visitation situation, but there are also responsibilities. Children must be given an etiquette for dealing with the various aspects of visitation, but this can only emerge after the parents and stepparents have developed their etiquette of step. Everyone in the situation should conform to a specific etiquette so that the process will run more smoothly.

The visiting parent (noncustodial) has a responsibility to the child that should, at the least, equal the good manners that you would show to an acquaintance:

Musts for the Visiting Parent

1. Do be on time when you pick up your child, and return him on time.

2. Do be at least cordial with your prior spouse. Your child should not have to start visitation with a tightened stomach.

3. Do clear your schedule so that you and your child can spend the time together.

4. Do integrate your child into the stepfamily.

5. Do call if you have to cancel or delay visitation.

6. Don't make last-minute changes of plans. These leave the child and everyone else hanging.

7. Don't demand to disrupt the established visitation schedule.

8. Don't pump your child for information about the other parent.

9. Don't flaunt your new partner in the other parent's face by taking him/her along when you pick up your child. If, however, there is an amiable relationship among all of the adults, then going together should create no friction.

10. Don't dump your child on the stepparent once you get home. If *your* child is visiting *you,* then you should stick around for a good part of the time.

The custodial parent also has a specific etiquette to follow in visitation:

Musts for the Custodial Parent

1. Do have your child ready on time for visitation.

2. Do make the experience of leaving for visitation as pleasant as possible for your child.

3. Do be cordial with your prior spouse, for the sake of the child's feelings.

4. Do let the child know that you will be busy while he is gone, not brooding.

5. Do call your prior spouse as early as possible if your child is ill or if visitation should be canceled for any reason.

6. Don't send your child out looking unkempt or without enough clothes for the weekend. Your intention may be to show how financially strapped you are, but you are punishing your child instead.

7. Don't send an ill child for visitation merely for the sake of convenience.

8. Don't tell your child that he can do anything he wishes during the visitation merely to spite the stepparent.

9. Don't pump your child for information as to how the other half lives.

10. Don't demand to change the visitation schedule, but negotiate when necessary.

Visitation must be planned and agreements must be kept. These are the golden rules of proper visitation. When those rules are broken, the child loses. Self-esteem is damaged and all parental relationships, both natural and step, are jeopardized.

The rights and responsibilities of the stepparent should also be clarified. Should you have to be there when your spouse's child visits? No. Too often the step partner is expected to fill the role of the absent biological parent. This puts too much pressure on the partner and creates tensions and resentments for everyone.

If your child is visiting, then it is your responsibility to be with the child in order to build your relationship. You can also help the two steps—parent and child—to establish a relationship that can grow at the rate that they desire. This, however, should not be considered the duty of the stepparent. Instead, the stepparent should also realize that nurturing the child is important. When you nurture the child, you also nurture the relationship.

These questions would not have arisen two decades ago. Even ten years ago, women easily accepted that it was a part of their duty to deal with the man's children during visitation. There was little concern regarding the step*father's* role when the woman's children visited, because most women retained custody.

Today's woman has a different attitude. The obligation is her husband's, and she lets him know it. Increasing numbers of stepparents want to handle their shopping, chores, and other weekend pursuits, not stay around for visitation. In the past, the father might have dumped the children in his home, then gone off to play tennis. He'd be out having fun while the stepmother would be in the kitchen baking cookies for children who insisted that Mommy's were better.

Even though the obligation is that of the biological parent, it is still better for the relationship if the stepparent spends time with the child and parent. Emotional etiquette prescribes that the stepparent be there for nearly half the visitation period, and certainly for dinners and Sunday brunch. The steppartner may pursue personal activities all day on Saturday. However the arrangements emerge, they must be determined by the parent and the stepparent as part of their decision-making responsibility.

Hellos and Good-byes, Please, and Thank You

Greetings, farewells, tones of voice, and telephone procedures are all important in stepfamilies. Intact families may ignore common courtesies in daily life, but if they are omitted in the stepfamily, rifts evolve.

A common complaint of many stepfamilies is that children do not say "hello" or "good-bye." In some cases, children and stepparents do not even talk to each other, and they seldom exchange more than a few words, even though they may live in the same home. Instead of complaining about this lack of courtesy, the implications of which go deep, both you and your partner should do something about it.

That something is to teach your children just how to behave in a courteous manner toward you, and to follow your own examples. Give the child a chance and a reason to say "hello" and "good-bye" to you. Greet the child with a "Hello, Mary," and see that Mary must now return a greeting and say, "Hello, John, Dad, or Pop," or whatever name has been chosen. Most have forgotten the rule, "The adult initiates the 'Hello,' the child must answer."

It is then your role to run with the ball. Ask the child how her day has been. Talk about the weather. Use whatever polite conversation comes to mind to draw the child out and to give her some direction for carrying out a conversation.

Silence among stepfamily members is ugly. It breeds misunderstanding. It also paralyzes the family and keeps members from sharing and growing together. Unfortunately, many adults don't want to take the initiative. They choose, instead, simply to blame each other, while the children continue to act rude and thoughtless. Step etiquette, and common courtesy, demand that the biological parent provides guidance, which has been agreed upon with the stepparent.

We often hear a lot of blaming in this situation. "You can't do anything with those children! They won't behave." "She overindulges her children, and she yells at me if I say anything!" That doesn't help the situation. If the adults don't establish the etiquette in the home, then those hellos and good-byes are never going to be heard.

Common courtesies such as "Hello," "Good-bye," "May I . . . ," "Please pass the vegetables," "Would you help me with this?" help to smooth the way and exhibit respect for each other.

Children must be taught that there are house rules to common courtesies and that ignoring them will have specific consequences. Consider the following exchange:

"Hello, Mary," says John, Mary's stepfather.

When he receives no reply, John repeats his greeting. "Mary, I said 'Hello.' In this household we say 'hello' to each other."

Mary replies. "I don't feel like it."

Upset by her refusal, John replies, "Mary, if you don't feel like saying 'hello,' it would be fine with me if you don't join us for dinner. You can eat in your room."

"Fine," Mary replies. "I don't care."

The adult is stymied.

The entire exchange served little purpose, except to push stepfather and stepdaughter further apart. Many adults feel the same frustration when they try to interact with children. There is often too much psychological distancing to overcome, and many adults feel that they have little ability or chance of success in delivering consequences to children. Since they fail to establish rules of etiquette in the home, and there are no clear-cut consequences for misbehavior, children continue to act erratically and to ignore common courtesies.

The adult has built up little victories while moving toward establishing step etiquette. In the above exchange, John should have considered himself the winner in round one when he told Mary directly that she is expected to say "hello" in their home. Enough said for that time. The consequences of not complying with the house rules should be well thought out in advance, however, or they will not achieve the desired results.

Sending Mary to her room to eat dinner was an act of anger that left John stymied and Mary satisfied. Had the consequence been withheld, Mary would have been at the dinner table and interacting, however minimally, with the family. As it was, she was banished. And John was shown to be the cruel stepfather.

You have to work to get the behavior that you want from a child. Anger is irrational and does not teach the child to become a social, well-mannered, and well-adjusted individual. A much better approach is to establish rules of etiquette, then use love, direction, and care to enforce these rules. The enforcer is the biological parent.

The Telephone

Telephone calls made both into and out of the step household can be a potent source of frayed nerves and difficult behavior. The everyday courtesy that may have been taken for granted in the 1950s has all but disappeared in the 1990s, and telephone calls have become prime examples of psychologically loaded communications.

For example, the former spouse may call, fail to identify herself, and ask the current spouse, who answers, "Is John there?" Who is she, anyway? Although such lapses in courtesy are common among many people when calling, this can be particularly irritating in the step household. The prior spouse should announce herself, then ask for John.

Children must also be given a telephone etiquette to follow when answering the phone in a step household. It can become pretty confusing. If Mom calls to speak with Dad, the child who answers the phone can simply say, "Dad, it's Mom on the phone."

What if the stepfather's former wife calls? The child should politely say "John, it's your former wife, Sally."

A stickier cause is when a noncustodial father calls his child and the stepfather answers. If you have straightened out all the naming in the household, and if everyone knows his niche, as all of you should, then common courtesy should handle it.

Ted, a noncustodial father, calls and wants to speak with his son. "Hi," he says. "This is Jimmy's father. I'd like to speak with him."

Dave, the stepfather, should cordially ask Ted to wait a moment, then call out to the child, "Jimmy, your father's on the phone and he'd like to speak with you." Finished. All of the characters have been identified and the conversation can follow.

If Jimmy is in another room, then Dave should go nearer to Jimmy to tell him that he has a call. Neither the parents nor the children should shout from one room to another. This is rude, disruptive, and not appropriate.

When children call into the step household to speak with their parent, other snubs occur. Rather than greet the stepmother or stepfather pleasantly when she or he answers the phone, many children will merely state their business: "Hello, I want to speak to Dad." No greeting. No pleasantries. That stepparent has reason to be annoyed. Making an issue of it with the child at that moment would probably do no good. But it should be dealt with.

The best way to deal with this lack of courtesy is to talk to the biological parent about it later. It is his/her role to reprimand the child.

He should mention the lack of greeting and tell the child, "When you call to speak with me and Sally answers, be friendly. Even if you don't mean it, you will say 'Hi, Sally, how are you? Is Dad there?' *Even if you don't mean it.*" Your tone of voice should get across to the child that *you* mean it.

One of the other common complaints is that when the former spouse calls, the husband "turns into a wimp" on the phone. In this case, it is best for the current wife to recognize that the prior spouse may have control over his children, and he is concerned that should he displease her in any way she will take it out of him through the children. The current wife should let it go and talk about it gently with him at some other time.

Telephoning Your Children When You Do Not Have Custody

We highly recommend that when the biological parent does not have custody, he or she call at least once or twice a week at a regular time. I cannot tell you how many adult parents have grown closer through our directive at the Stepfamily Foundation that telephone dates be made at specific times or that children be given the right to call collect.

Who Sees the Teacher?

There are no ex-parents, only ex-spouses. Both parents should know how their child is doing in school and they should both have the opportunity to meet with teachers when problems exist in the child's school performance. Report cards, parents' night invitations, and parent-teacher conference requests should be received by both parents so that they can both participate fully in their child's life. If you are not being given equal notification of your child's progress, you have the legal right to request that the school begin giving it to you immediately.

Even if you have remarried and are not the custodial parent, you are *still* the parent. That means that both natural parents should attend school functions. You may sit apart, but your presence is important to your child. Your child should feel confident that even if only one of you has custody, *both* of you are concerned about him.

What about the stepparents? Should they also attend school functions?

Before you can answer this, you should examine the role that the stepparent plays in the child's daily life. The child who lives with his father and a stepmother or with his mother and a stepfather will naturally have greater daily contact with that stepparent than with the noncustodial stepparent. He will be helped with homework, guided through test anxieties, and be given more advice by the inhouse stepparent. For that reason, there may be a strong justification for that stepparent's going to school functions with the parent.

The same cannot be said of the spouse of the noncustodial parent who often has little, if any, daily contact with the child and who has no involvement in his daily schoolwork. There is no reason for that stepparent to attend a school function, unless it is simply for the purpose of being present. And this is not necessarily a good reason.

Before a collection of prior and present spouses decides to show up at the child's school, find out how the child feels. Then do what's best for the child. The egos of the adults should not be the deciding factor.

Many areas of the step relationship cannot depend upon traditional family etiquette to guide the actions of the stepfamily members. Visitation, the issue of holidays, family interaction, and other factors require new rules. This chapter on step etiquette should give you some answers. But be prepared to find your own answers to the unpredictable situations that crop up in step—and use your common sense.

Chapter 15

A BABY, MAYBE?

Living with stepchildren for a few years has made many stepmothers and stepfathers who have never parented vow that they would never want to have a child of their own. For others, the opposite is true. The urge to produce a biological child is strengthened by their stepparenting role. The choice and decision differ according to the nature of the step relationship and the obligations of the adults.

To Conceive or Not to Conceive

Even when the two adults in the stepfamily agree on other issues in the marriage, they may diverge widely on the issue of producing more children. When both have children running around the home or when one is paying the emotional and financial prices of having children who are being raised by a prior spouse, it's understandable why they might be emphatically against the idea of producing still more children. Yet, many couples in step relationships do wish to have more children.

In some cases, a man or woman who has not had children marries a man or woman with children. These stepchildren may draw out the parenting urges of the stepparent and make the desire to have a child irresistible. For women who have been building their careers and who wait until their early thirties to marry, the desire to have a child may well accompany the decision to marry. It is their right—and they also become extremely aware of the biological time clock.

Men who have never parented, but who marry a woman with children, may find their own parenting urges also coming out. They may discover that nurturing has its own great rewards, and they want some more of the experience. As their stepchildren grow older, they will begin to feel more urgently the need to produce a baby and to have a child around with whom to play out their nurturing impulses. They see having a child of their own as *their* natural right.

The couple may jointly desire a child for any number of reasons. For some, the creation of a child is a necessary part of every marriage. In some mythic way, creating a child with your spouse validates the marriage and the relationship. For others, the need to put the stamp of approval on the marriage lies in having a baby together. Still others see babymaking as a testimonial to their continued sexual potency. The baby becomes positive proof that they are still sexually attractive and sexually active.

For every couple that desires to create a baby who is both of theirs, there is a step couple who is horrified at the thought.

One woman who had never parented grimaced when asked if she wanted to have a baby with her new spouse. "A baby?" she replied. "I've had enough of parenting to last a lifetime. No, make that two lifetimes. His daughters are here every weekend and, because I work all week, I barely get to spend any time with him. They're demanding, ill-natured, and selfish. No. No more children for me. I can't wait until they grow up." The girls are fourteen and sixteen years of age.

Others who had never parented before entering a step relationship exhibit a similar reluctance. "Why should we have a baby?" asked one man. "She has spoon-fed the one she has. She barely has time for me. Where would she fit in time to meet the demands of an infant?"

The Mid-Thirties Career Woman and a Baby Maybe?

Never before have we witnessed a time when so many women in their mid-thirties are having babies. Indeed, we are seeing a mid-thirties baby boom. At the same time, we are seeing millions of women choosing not to have children.

Many of these women in their thirties have delayed marriage to further their career aspirations. When the time comes to marry, the marriage frequently involves an older man who is divorced with children of his own.

So, first we see these women becoming stepmothers to his children, and then the issue of children of their own must be dealt with.

In 1970 we at the Stepfamily Foundation experienced a 70 percent increase in the number of women who live in step and who were facing the dilemma of a Baby Maybe.

Many of the couples had agreed to have a baby before the marriage. Others had not completely dealt with the predicament posed by having a baby.

Once the couple experience some of the traumas of step, ideas about their own baby may change. In addition, the couple will need the income of both partners to continue their current life style. Her income will be needed. Yet, she wants a child of her own.

Often the husband changes his mind when he sees her having problems with his children. Meanwhile, her biological clock continues to run, and her paycheck continues to come in.

This is the time to seek counseling. We have successfully solved this vital issue with hundreds of women in their thirties and forties. Issues such as time often need to be carefully worked out. Take a look back at the tools, Chapter 6.

Time. That is a factor that many people who are in step relationships often mention when explaining why they don't want to have children. The children in their home already require substantial attention, and the adults fear losing even more time with each other.

Money is another factor that frequently arises in the decision to have or not to have a baby. According to the Bureau of Vital Statistics, raising a child to the age of twenty-one can cost more than $350,000. That's a chunk to consider. Even divided up over twenty-one years, and allowing for error, the cost of having and raising a child can be phenomenal.

More aware of the cost of children may be the parent who is paying alimony and child support for his noncustodial children. Each month, or however often he makes out the check, that parent is reminded that raising children is expensive. A ruptured marriage is also costly.

Energy is another element to factor into your decision. Children need not only our time and money, but a tremendous amount of energy. Consider the time and energy demands on today's working woman, or man. Consider the extended family and household help available to the nonworking woman of the fifties. Now look at the energy, planning, focus and responsibility needed for a baby today. The emotional impact of these issues will be looked at historically. Today we must just weigh them and deal with them. (Personally, I rank "Mother" on the top of the list of my career accomplishments—but that is something everyone must decide for him or herself.)

Even emotional losses come into consideration in the decision to have a baby. Noncustodial parents, mother or father, may be even more reluctant to have more children than parents whose children are living in the stepfamily. They are already wrestling with the guilt of their first family, even if they see their children regularly.

Creating another child will mean that this child will be in the step household, and will have two parents. The first set of children do not. If the other parent has remarried, they will, at best, have only one biological parent and one stepparent on the premises.

Time, money, and energy all create strong fears in parents and stepparents when they consider having a child of their own. Some of the debris of the former marriage must be cleared away before a decision is made. Use the following questions as a guide:

1. Do you really *want* to have a baby?
2. Are you physically strong enough not only to produce a child but also to deal with the broken nights and the anxiety of infant care?
3. Can you *afford* to have a baby and to raise the child, in light of your future obligations to the already existing children?
4. Are you willing to give up the time that raising an infant will require?
5. What are your reasons for wanting a baby?
6. How do you feel that a baby of this marriage will affect the existing children?

Certainly, one obvious result of creating a child of the marriage is that you effectively tell the world, and your children, both natural and biological, that this marriage is real. It is not just a temporary relationship, but one in which you are making a significant commitment. This last aspect is one that may be most upsetting to your children.

The Effect on Existing Children

Stepchildren tend to view the stepparent who has never parented as either a temporary occupant or as the new help in the family. Stepdaddy who comes with no children can easily be ignored as he goes to work daily and returns home at night. His paycheck may be his most notable characteristic.

Stepmommy probably works, but she is also saddled with the care and feeding of the family, unless wise precautions and structuring exist. They are, in effect, players in the stepfamily drama. Their only tie to the household is in the marriage to the children's parent.

The stepparent who brings children into the household has a strong tie with the stepfamily because some of her offspring make up the relationship. Someone who has parented is also more assertive in gaining the cooperation and assistance of all the children of the household. She or he is experienced with children and may be seen as less of a pushover than the nonparent.

What happens when the parent and the stepparent create a child who belongs not to one set of step siblings or to the other, but to both? Insecurity sets in. The baby validates the marriage. While every child, aside from the baby, has only one biological parent in the home, the new baby has two. Further, when people who have never parented produce children, they undergo a change of image. They are now *parents*.

Stepchildren may feel threatened. How will this new sibling affect the emotional sharing? Who will come first? How will discipline be handled? Where do the existing children fit into the new ordering of the stepfamily household?

The birth of a child can evoke many of the same fears that children experience when the stepfamily is first formed when the parent marries. There will be a new pecking order. Areas of responsibility will change. Insecurity may begin to creep in.

Both the parent and the stepparent have to, once again, take control of the situation. The stepchildren may well view the baby as an intruder on their turf, who is related to none of them. Yet, this is false. A baby born of the step relationship is very much a part of *both* families. He carries the blood of both families and, as a result, can very logically be viewed as a link between the two entities.

It is up to the parents to positively condition the already existing children to the arrival of the new child. This is traditionally done in a number of ways. Assure the child that he or she is the firstborn son or daughter. Tell the children how important they will be in helping you deal with the new baby. The existing children will be the big sister or the big brother to the new baby. Tell them that they are major factors in the pleasures of bringing a new life into this world.

Very often the new baby will be several years younger than the existing children. Therefore, the issues that come to the fore are ones of assistance, caring, and help. The important idea is that we are going to bring this new life into the family, together.

In the many people we counsel we have found the new birth to be a positive one when the children are conditioned and prepared. The older child now becomes a helpmate, and the baby becomes a learning experience. It is important to relate to the children that this is their own flesh and blood. The idea of a tiny new brother or sister often excites the children and serves to unify the stepfamily.

The stepfamily that is in trouble should not decide on having a baby with the hope that the baby will provide the badly needed unifying factor. That rarely works in nonstep marriages. Before the decision to create a baby is made, the step couple has to have the family running smoothly. You already know what that requires.

Every member of the family, the parent, stepparent, biological children, and stepchildren, should know what is expected of them. They should know their job descriptions. Family rules, regulations, and requirements should also be known by everyone in the stepfamily. The consequences for violating these should be posted.

It is only when the mechanism of the step relationship has been established that you should think of bringing another child into the fold. A baby can disrupt your lives, stress everyone, and make you miserable. On the other hand, a baby can also be the symbol that the stepfamily has merged into a family.

Chapter 16

THE VITAL GENERATION: GRANDPARENTS

In the hectic business that surrounds divorce and remarriage, the roles played by grandparents and other relatives in the child's extended family are often forgotten. This is unfortunate, because the child continues to need the warmth and love that these other relatives can provide, beyond their natural parents. In many cases, the child loses all contact with the grandparents or other family from the noncustodial side of the family. Even if this is not the case right after the divorce, it often becomes the rule when the custodial parent remarries.

As a rule grandparents fare badly in the step situation. So do their grandchildren if the two are pulled apart. Grandparents are valuable to the child because they represent a special kind of love.

A Special Kind of Love

Grandparents usually adore their grandchildren without asking first if they are getting good grades in school and without checking whether they have straightened out their rooms. The love and sharing of grandparents with their grandchildren is a combination of warmth, doting, caretaking, pride, and concern. When we take away a child's grandparents, we take away plenty.

Although the wishes of the biological parent have traditionally dictated the extent that grandparents may visit grandchildren, this is changing. The courts are beginning to recognize the psychological value of continuity in a child's life, and grandparents are an important part of this.

Dealing with Divorce

Sons and daughters are often uncomfortable about discussing their divorces and remarriages with parents. In the grandparents' generation, divorce didn't exist. Or, if it did, it wasn't talked about . . . It is a great trauma for them, for their child who is divorcing, for their grandchildren.

There are a variety of problems that the grandparents must confront, especially when the divorce has occurred after a long marriage. For years, the grandparents may have thought of and treated their son's wife as their own daughter. When divorce occurs, however, they are expected abruptly to sever the tie and to change their feelings. The trauma is compounded when their child remarries and they have now to accept a new daughter-in-law, who comes to them with no shared history. She may also come to them with a few children whom the grandparents are expected to welcome into their home. This may occur while their natural grandchildren are being kept from them, and their hearts are breaking.

Respecting the Long-Term Bonds

Thus, the grandparents experience serious trauma in both the divorce and the remarriage. Older grandparents may have formed so strong a bond over the years that their sympathies lie with the old in-law. As they give their sympathies to their child's former spouse, they may effectively alienate their own child.

With divorce and remarriage, issues such as holidays, traditions, birthdays, and special occasions are increasingly complex. What happens to Christmas at Grandma's when the divorce occurs and Grandma is the parent of the noncustodial parent? How do you handle this?

How do we accommodate the parents of the new partner in the step relationship who may want to have the step grandchildren begin to think of them as grandparents? Is it fair for the child to add another set of grandparents to his collection? Should we drop one set of grandparents to make room?

How does keeping contact with the parents of the prior spouse, the natural grandparents of the child, affect the stepfamily relationship? Will a current spouse be resentful?

Who do you invite to family parties? Who comes to weddings? What about funerals? The etiquette in this area is nonexistent.

What happens when the grandparent who has become attached to both the old in-law and the new in-law falls ill? Many hospitals only permit *immediate family* to see seriously ill patients. Who is permitted?

The problems multiply.

There is also the issue of step grandparents to consider. When their children remarry and their new spouses have young children, the stage is set for strong bonding between the children and their new step grandparents. Should such relationships break up, the step grandparent is effectively barred from seeing these children.

This, however, may be changing, as the courts begin to rely

more heavily on determining what is in the best interests of the child, and as they consider more the emotional and psychological bonds.

The Growing Rights of Grandparents

Angelo T. Cometa, of Phillips, Nizer, Benjamin, Krim & Ballon, and Harriet Newman Cohen, of Cohen, Hennessey & Bienstock and author of *The Divorce Book for Men and Women,* are the attorneys for the Stepfamily Foundation. They note that there is a growing trend in the courts toward recognizing the right of grandparents to visit their grandchildren. Decisions are made based on the way in which the "benefits to the child from visitation with a grandparent" would emerge from the continued contact with the grandparents.

Step grandparents can't even hope for that much.

Certainly, the situation would be better all around if the adults in the step situation could objectively and lovingly look at the various complexities from the viewpoint of their children. If the "benefits to the children" dominated their decision-making, much of the pain of step might be eliminated.

Chapter 17

LEGAL RIGHTS IN STEP

What are your legal obligations as a stepparent? Where are your rights? Do you have any rights in regard to your stepchildren? What about support payments? Debts? Wills?

What is commonly done at the Stepfamily Foundation is that prenuptial, and even postnuptial, marital agreements are worked out in counseling sessions. It is our belief that this is a more elegant, less expensive, and less painful way for partners to agree on the legal aspects of their remarriage. After each issue has been discussed, fought about, and finally agreed to, with the help of one of our professional counselor/mediators, we then direct the couple to formalize the agreement with their attorneys. Legally each is required to retain a separate attorney.

Both Angelo T. Cometa and Harriet Newman Cohen, attorneys, recommend that most couples entering step marriages see a lawyer and have a *prenuptial agreement* drawn up. If you are already married, it is not too late to draw up a marriage contract, known as a postnuptial agreement. It is important to the new step partnership to know exactly the financial obligations, assets, and responsibilities—past, present, and future.

Ten Steps to Prenuptial and Other Marriage Contracts

1. Read and understand prior divorce agreements: the implications for each. Ascertain financial obligations, his, hers, and theirs. Note changes upon remarriage. For example, alimony payments, payments to cease upon remarriage, or should his income increase, the former wife's payments are also increased, which may decrease the new wife's financial rights, should there be no prenuptial. According to Cohen, using percentages may be unwise. It may be best to use dollar amounts, depending on the facts.

2. Delineate total current income and expenditures. Current alimony and child support payments and related costs. Current living expenses.

3. Anticipated costs of remarriage, *e.g.,* purchase of new home, construction, life insurance, etc. Costs of a Baby Maybe?

4. Agree upon division of expenses and responsibilities. It is important and complicated to decide on the dollar amount in case of divorce. Counselor and attorney work best to advise you here.

5. Decide what is to be owned individually and what jointly. Note that these decisions may change or be reviewed.

6. Develop a 3-, 5-, and 7-year plan. For example, you may want a spouse who owns a house to allow the other partner to become part-owner, even 50-percent owner, over the course of the marriage. Let us say s/he would "vest" to half ownership in seven years.

7. Decide on the disposition of assets in case of death, *e.g.,* home, insurance policies, IRAs, etc.

8. Decide on the disposition of assets in case of divorce. One way to prepare for this issue is for the couple to maintain separate checking accounts, perhaps a joint "house" account with each contributing money to that account to pay expenses. This avoids "commingling" moneys, which may indicate, in case of divorce without a prenuptial, that your intention was to merge your incomes; "What is mine is yours," etc. In case of a divorce, you would stand little chance of recovering any extraordinary expenditures.

9. Check laws applicable in all states that might be involved.

10. Get prenuptial, postnuptial, or living-together counseling.

Your Financial Obligations in Step

Most step couples consist of two working partners, and new wives have become increasingly aware of their role in keeping the family financially solvent. Their husbands may be paying out large amounts of alimony and child support, and it becomes the wife's role to supply the money for the new household. Is she obligated to underwrite his alimony and support obligations? Of course not! But often she does just that. Without a prenuptial, she might be legally obligated to support his children, had she set that precedent by not limiting her obligation through a legal marital agreement.

What about the obligations of the stepparent to the children who live in the same household?

If the biological parents are able to support their child, then the law looks upon support as their responsibility. However, when the parent who is obligated to support the child dies, disappears, or goes broke, the law starts looking around for someone else to assume the responsibility. They may turn to the stepparent before recommending public assistance.

Although not all states have made the move, some have already initiated legislation that will hold stepparents liable for support of their stepchildren in cases where the biological parents lack sufficient funds. As Angelo Cometa points out, this liability is long-term and may continue until the child is twenty-one years old. However, the responsibility will only be imposed *if* both biological parents have insufficient funds *and* the child is on the brink of becoming a public charge. Harriet N. Cohen notes the child support obligation for a stepchild that arises out of what is called a "promissory estoppel." She says, "If you promise to support, in words or deeds, the courts may legally have the right to reach into the stepparent's income, unless a marital agreement defines the issue otherwise."

In some cases, the stepparent may avoid this responsibility if a prenuptial or postnuptial agreement has established that the partners of the marriage kept separate financial identities. His money is his. Her money is hers. What about the children? It is something to consider.

There are a variety of circumstances that make the issue of support and the stepparent difficult. If the stepparent does not know about the stepchildren at the time of the marriage, then he or she will *most likely* not be liable to support the children during the marriage. *However,* once a stepparent does commit himself to support the stepchildren and begins to act publicly in the role of parent, a tricky liability game emerges. Should the couple separate, the stepparent is not relieved of his duty, even if he does not have custody or visitation with the child. The two, support and visitation, are distinct issues. "Visitation with a step after divorce is usually by consent," says Ms. Cohen, "not by court order."

In general, a stepparent's financial liability for stepchildren terminates when a divorce occurs between the step and the biological parents. But this is not a strict rule. In some stepfamilies, a stepparent assumes the role of parent to the point that all contact with the biological parent is ended and the children actually feel that the individual is their father or mother. When this is the case, and when the children have been led to expect the stepparent to be relied upon and treated as a natural parent, the courts may well rule that divorce cannot sever either those emotional or those financial ties. In this case, the stepparent may become liable for support.

Inheritance/Wills

The safest way to ensure that everyone you love will get the amount of your estate that you wish is to have a will drawn up and update it regularly. Without a will, the laws of your state will allocate what you leave behind by rigid and sometimes inequitable statutory principles, no matter how close you may have been to your stepchildren and others. As Angelo Cometa points out, you can be financially responsible for stepchildren, yet you can't automatically leave them something without prior planning. Only biological children or those who were legally adopted can be the beneficiary of parents who die without a will.

You should seriously reflect on this possibility. If you want to leave money, property, or other tangible items to your stepchildren, you should have a will drawn up that spells out your desires. And keep in mind that a will can be changed as your family and your feelings change. You should review your will regularly, and *especially* after you remarry.

Should you die without a will, your current spouse will be allocated a percentage of the estate and the rest will be shared among your natural and legally adopted children. Your prior spouse, in this case, gets nothing. Depending on the state where you live, your current spouse may automatically inherit up to half of the estate. The children, even if they have been living with the prior spouse for all of the time, may only share the other half.

Stepparents and Visitation

There have been too many cases of stepparents who invest many years in raising stepchildren only to find that they have no legal rights for further contact once the marriage fails. For the most part, stepparents have little, if any, legal right to visitation if the natural parent denies them that right. In some cases, the stepchild will work to convince the natural parent to allow visits, or the stepchild will take the initiative once he is old enough to visit on his own.

The problem may be alleviated through a redefinition of the term "parent." In California, the law uses the concept of the "psychological parent," whether it be a grandparent, stepparent, adoptive parent, or the biological parent, as the determining factor in visitation issues. However enlightened, this law is limited in that the right of visitation in these cases can only be initiated while the divorce is in process, not afterward.

To come to terms with this important issue, Angelo Cometa and Harriet Cohen suggest that the stepparent act during the dissolution of the marriage to secure visitation through negotiation. Cometa suggests that a stepparent may secure a visitation privilege to a stepchild by using it as a bargaining tool in the dissolution proceedings. You could request this right in the separation papers. Cohen adds that the courts, in this instance, may, depending on the facts and circumstances, look favorably toward a contractual agreement between parties where the right of visitation is granted to the stepparent by the natural parent. Sadly, in our experience since 1975 in the divorces we have witnessed and/or mediated, stepparents are often discarded by their former stepfamily after the divorce. Stepparents, who may have devoted years and years of time, money, and energy to their stepchildren, only seldom end up having a postdivorce relationship with them.

In some cases, the stepparent may also petition the court that visitation would be in the best interest of the stepchild, particularly when the focus is on the psychological factors arising out of an excellent stepparent-child relationship.

Planning for the Legal Unpredictables

Some stepparents worry about their role if the natural parent is absent. Can I still discipline the child? Of course, and use the discussions on discipline already presented to guide you. The key is that all discipline must be *reasonable*. Corporal punishment even by natural parents has been called into question in recent years.

What about obtaining medical assistance or admitting a stepchild to the hospital? Parents should plan for the unforeseen. Injuries could occur while the stepparent is alone with the stepchild. Not having the right to admit the child to a hospital is dangerous to the child. Straightening this out is a simple matter. Just have the natural parent submit a note to both the child's school and doctor, together with a general "to whom it may concern" letter, each of which states that you, the stepparent, have the right to act on the behalf of the natural parent.

There is a growing body of stepparents in this nation, and many of them are becoming increasingly concerned about their legal rights and responsibilities. Because of this, the next few decades should see substantial lobbying and change in legislation to accommodate their emerging needs.

Chapter 18

JOINT CUSTODY: TRENDY BUT TRICKY

It does not take a sage or a prophet to know that families are rapidly changing in America. Step families are also changing. Up until a few years ago, joint custody was *not* an issue. Recently, it has become more and more an accepted fashion of handling custody after divorce. The intention of joint custody, from our point of view, is for both parents to assume equal responsibility for the children. Joint custody has been heralded as an exciting new way of not forcing children to choose and taking away the mandate that mothers are routinely awarded custody of the children. Fathers, in the past because they worked and were not home, rarely received custody of their children. But with more and more women working this has all changed.

Joint custody was begun as an experiment in the late sixties. At least thirty states have replaced traditional sole-custody laws with joint-custody statutes—and legislation is pending in many other states.

The labels vary—"joint parenting," "co-parenting," "joint custody"—but all pertain to a judge's ordering both parents to share in the rearing of the children. Another kind of court order can require only joint legal custody, wherein parents only share in the major decisions, and it may or may not include joint physical custody of the child.

A typical situation in joint custody might look something like this: the child spends Mondays through Wednesdays with the mother, shifts houses on Wednesday night, and then spends Wednesday through Friday with the father. Weekends are alternated, as are holidays.

Many organizations, such as the National Organization of Women, are opposed to joint custody, labeling it as a method by which the fathers are not forced to pay appropriate amounts of child support. Controversy around joint custody rages back and forth.

A Joint Custody Case That Works: The Taylors

In our experience at the Stepfamily Foundation, joint custody can be a very wonderful solution, especially where parents live close to each other and have a good working relationship with each other. The children feel less of a loss and feel that they have both parents in separate and different ways. In one family that we worked with, the Taylors, joint custody has worked probably the best we have ever seen it. In the Taylor family, young Mary and Timothy go back and forth between their mother's and father's houses in a Connecticut suburb with their nanny. What seems to make this situation work out the best is that the nanny travels with the children and adds to the children's feeling of security. Both Mr. and Mrs. Taylor work at substantial jobs and can afford equal sets of clothes, equal kinds of housing, and equal pay for the maid and private school situation. Both Mr. Taylor and the ex-Mrs.

Taylor have new people in their lives. The children seem to accept this without many of the conflicts that surround divorce and step relationships—we believe largely because of the nanny, who acts as a traveling mother figure and is a stabilizing influence on these children. In addition, the step people—Mr. Taylor's new lady and Mrs. Taylor's new man—do not have to deal with these children on a full-time visitation basis, as many people do in joint custody. The nanny and the other person resource is there to help the children with their homework, handle their clothes, do their washing, chauffeur them, and do the daily parenting in the course of their daily step parenting tasks. This is vital in making the situation work.

This is a good news story about step and joint custody. But unfortunately, not everyone has the money to afford a full-time nanny.

The Constant Reshuffle

We also see many joint custody arrangements that are not as fruitful and perfect as the Taylors'. The main problem that we see in joint custody is step, whether the couple is married or unmarried. How is joint custody different than weekend visitation or every-other-weekend visitation? It's predictable, and there's more of it, and very often there are more logistics involved. These logistics have to be very carefully worked out by the biological parents. Otherwise the stepparents may become the managers of the joint custody. Of course, we see many instances like this where conflicts arise over the resentment of having his/her children invade their household for three days. The dust is just beginning to settle and they reinvade for another three days. This happens very often at the beginning of joint custody, but it may go on for too-long periods of time. The situation becomes further entangled if the step partner has his/her own visiting children. Joint custody can be a logistical quagmire.

A child could be the oldest in one household and the youngest in another. Children may play one parent against the other. They may unconsciously feel able to control two households.

Certainly, as the end child, when I traveled between my mother's house and my father's house, I felt myself to be the center of attention—the most important element in each one of those households. I am not sure that this is in keeping with good parenting. It gives the child too much of a sense of power. Fortunately, my parents were loving disciplinarians and I fared much better than I might have.

Joint custody, in short, may not be suitable for all those who idealize it as the perfect solution. Seek advice. Weigh the pros and cons. Joint custody should be carefully planned. It should be evaluated by an outside source, such as the Stepfamily Foundation. The purpose is to maintain the best emotional health of the parent, the child, and the step relating individuals involved. Those are the criteria upon which we base a decision for joint custody. Different kinds of joint custody may be negotiated. For example, joint custody can involve one parent's taking the child during the school year and another parent's taking the child for vacation times. We have worked this out quite well with many families.

Change of Custody

All too many stepparents have remarried someone who did not have custody of the children, usually the man, and discovered that a legal custody battle is in process. Or that the new partner has asked for custody and is about to receive it. Sometimes this can be a very cruel event for a stepparent and can create a great deal of resentment, because the step dynamics take place without proper preparation. It is vital for a couple seeking to change present custody carefully to work out their emotional, psychological, financial, and time management responses to this new and vital element. Too often custody changes occur before the stepparent really knows what's about to happen. The results can be disastrous for everyone involved. Or if carefully planned and thought through, they may fulfill your highest hopes and visions for the good of the child.

Money

Another issue that is vital in co-parenting situations is to prorate the financial contributions of both parents. In many cases that we have seen, in co-parenting and joint custody the expenses are divided up equally between the mother and the father. Still, most women earn only 60 percent of what men do and may earn even less, having devoted much of their time during the marriage to child rearing, or supporting the male career. In the case of the Steins—a couple we worked with—Mrs. Stein earned $20,000 a year, while Mr. Stein earned over $100,000 a year. They got along well and agreed to equal financial responsibilities of time and energy and money for their one son, Sam. As Mr. Stein moved up the corporate ladder, he found he had less and less time for Sam. It was left to ex-wife Mrs. Stein to take on more and more custody of the child, with no increase in her monies from her ex-husband. When he remarried, pressures from his new wife and pressures from his job, influenced him to opt for his new family and job, and he decreased his visitations with Sam. This became a very complicated situation, which we had to unwind and mediate and financially settle. The Bible says the road to hell is paved with good intentions. We, as responsible parents, must carefully plan our joint custody arrangements but not cast them in legal cement. What works today may not work tomorrow. It is in the best interests of everyone to stay flexible.

Chapter 19

THE ART OF POSITIVE THINKING

Jane was married to a judge. He was powerful and sometimes bombastic, but underneath he was a real sweetheart of a guy. When she wanted something from him, she didn't complain or berate him for his deficiencies. She planted the behavior she desired. It went something like this: We were sitting at a dinner table with friends and Jane began to talk about how wonderful the judge was. How brilliant, how wise . . . She talked about sitting in the back of his beautiful courtroom and looking at him, "the big muckety-muck judge," while he worked—how proud she was to be his wife.

She spoke lovingly. He beamed. Then she went on to plant the behavior she desired—how he always bought her flowers. (He hadn't bought her flowers for a year.) How he brought her candy. How he was so dear with her kids. (He wasn't so sure he always liked them.) How he thanked her for the things she did for his children. (He hadn't.) The judge began to look wide-eyed and a bit embarrassed. He knew he hadn't done any of those things. Jane continued.

Jane was a therapist and had learned a new technique called "future pacing." She was practicing it on her husband. She was joyfully assuming a behavior that she wanted to get and planting it by talking about it. She knew what she was doing. The judge knew what she was doing too, and the group was entertained.

Jane went on to regale the group with his tendernesses and caring. The judge began to enjoy the story and to smile. Being an honorable man, he, of course, felt obliged to live up to all these praisings. And he did.

There are literally hundreds of books on positive thinking. Read them. We cannot stress how important it is in a step relationship to envision, think, and assume positively. It is my belief that what we envision is often what we create. The Bible says, "So a man thinketh, so he is." Other teachers of mine have said, "thoughts are creative." Step is fraught with unpredictable and negative behavior. The potential for explosive interaction lurks in the most mundane of everyday transactions. Should we allow our feelings of inattention, resentment unreceived, and expected behavior to dominate our step relationship, we embark upon the classic negatives of step.

One tool that we urge is that of actually envisioning the outcome that we want and discussing this with our spouse or lover, thereby creating two visions, two goals of the desired outcome, whether that outcome is about the visit of children, the laying down of discipline, or the simple things that we want from each other in this relationship.

Taking this all a bit further is the use of what I call "assuming the positive." In my business background I was taught that "to ASS U ME makes an ass out of you and me." In my practice of working with thousands of individuals, I have found that a valuable tool is to teach people to assume—that is, to assume the positive. As we've just seen, sometimes when we assume the behavior we want, we get it. It's the art of diplomacy—and even, yes, positive manipulation. We may have lost this art in these recent decades of extreme "tell it like it is" honesty. In my opinion, we have become so direct and often so negative with each other that our upsets and our anger about events only succeed in getting us the opposite of what we want. But with the use of a positive vision and a good attitude, we can very often motivate others and get the results we want.

Whether you began this book as a stepparent or as someone about to enter a step relationship, remember that the stepfamily can be a warm and loving refuge from the world. As with anything important to our lives, however, it doesn't come easy. You have to want the relationship to succeed, then structure your stepfamily life in a way that it *will* succeed.

All through this book, we have emphasized the fact that the adults, the stepparent and the parent, have the responsibility for creating the job descriptions of family members, for establishing the rules and regulations of the stepfamily, and for creating the standards for discipline.

If you are about to enter a step relationship, you must talk honestly with your partner and come to an agreement about the way your stepfamily should be run. Go back to Chapter 6 and compare your responses to the tools for assessing your notion of the family and the way in which it should be run. If you disagree in certain areas, discuss those disagreements and come to a reasonable compromise. Then you can create the structure that will provide your new step relationship with the unity it needs.

If you are already in a step relationship and feel that certain areas are unsatisfactory, those same tools can help you to determine the problem areas. Even if you have lived in the same household for three years, you may not view family roles in the same way, and you may not have the same perspective on contributions by each partner.

Discuss your differences and compromise. Think positively. You *want* it to work. Your children and stepchildren *need* to have it work. Communicate with each other, and you'll find that it *will* work.

It's also wise for most steps to get educational counseling.

The Stepfamily Foundation, 333 West End Avenue, New York, N.Y. provides memberships, information short term counseling, and telephone counseling nationwide. The telephone number is (212) 877-3244. The 24-hour information line is (212) 799-STEP. The Crisis Hotline is (212) 744-6924.

To order memberships and fax-packets particular to your specific issues call 1-800-SKY STEP, 9-5 EST. (Have your credit card ready.)